KING AND OUTLAW

THE REAL ROBERT THE BRUCE

CHRIS BROWN

CHRIS BROWN has taught medieval history for St Andrews and Edinburgh universities, appeared as consultant on numerous documentaries, and conducts heritage tours at battlefield sites. He is the author of *William Wallace: The Man and the Myth* and *Bannockburn 1314: The Battle 700 Years On* (both The History Press). Unsurprisingly, he is highly regarded as an expert on fourteenth-century Scottish history.

Cover illustration: Martin Latham

First published 2018
This paperback edition published 2020

The History Press
97 St George's Place, Cheltenham
Gloucestershire, GL50 3QB
www.thehistorypress.co.uk

British Library Cataloguing in Publication Data.
A catalogue record for this book is available from the British Library.

ISBN 978 0 7509 9392 0

Typesetting and origination by The History Press
Printed and bound in Great Britain by TJ International Ltd

CONTENTS

INTRODUCTION

Without question Robert the Bruce is Scotland's most famous king and one of the great figures of his time. It is often assumed – even asserted – that we do not really know a great deal about him.

What most people *think* they know about Robert the Bruce is:

He was born in Essex in 1274.

He was a French-speaking Anglo-Norman with enormous estates in England.

He was the rightful heir to Alexander III, but Edward I appointed John Balliol as king in his stead.

He betrayed William Wallace at the battle of Falkirk and scored one victory over Edward II on a boggy hillside at Bannockburn with his band of ill-equipped peasants.

He died of leprosy in 1327.

None of this is true, but it is what people believe. Robert was indeed born in 1274 and he did die in 1327, but the rest can be neatly defined as 'codswallop'.

Robert's road to the throne was a long struggle – he had to fight two civil wars against domestic opposition as well as dislodge the English occupation. After the Battle of Bannockburn in June 1314 he was finally master of his kingdom, but the war would drag on for more than a decade before he managed to force a treaty that recognised his kingship and Scotland's independence. Unfortunately he had little opportunity to enjoy the fruits of his labours, as he died in 1329.

However, we know that he was an educated man; he was fond of the kind of tales medieval people called 'Romances' and delighted in reading about the exploits of ancient kings and warriors. His activity is recorded in the stream of documents he issued – letters, instructions, charters, court cases, warrants, appointments and responses – nearly all of which give us both a location and a date, allowing us to track his whereabouts and actions on an almost day-to-day basis.

This book's purpose is not to examine or explain why there have been so many myths concocted about Robert the Bruce, nor why they have endured so. Instead it aims to provide an accessible guide to Robert's life and the circumstances he overcame to become one of the great kings and commanders of the medieval era.

1

A MAN WHO WOULD BE KING

Despite his Norman name, when Robert Bruce was born on 11 July 1274 he was about as Scottish as a child could be. His father's family held the Lordship of Annandale and had been resident in Scotland for five generations, and his mother Marjorie was the Countess of Carrick – an ancient Celtic earldom.

Oddly, his career was formed by the choices of his greatest enemy, Edward I. If Edward had not been an exceptionally greedy man, he would not have forced the candidates for Scottish kingship to accept him as their overlord in 1290–91. John Balliol would still have been chosen as king – this was not Edward's decision to make, but Edward would not have been in a position to undermine him and force a war. There is no reason to think that John would not have been a perfectly adequate ruler or that the Bruce family would have done any-thing more exciting than carry on with being Earls of Carrick and Lords of Annandale. Had it not been for Edward's violent avarice, the name Robert Bruce would be known to a tiny handful of academic spe-cialists, and no one else.

At the time of Scottish King Alexander III's death in 1286, Scotland and England had enjoyed a long tradition of fairly good relations. Intermittent attempts by English kings over the preceding two centuries and more to procure a degree of sovereignty over Scottish counterparts had never really taken root; indeed, it is questionable whether any English king had ever seriously believed that they would. William the Lion (reigned 1165–1214) had been obliged to give homage for his kingdom after he was captured in 1174 as part of his ransom arrangements, but fifteen years later he paid a large sum to ensure that he and his successors would be free of any feudal obligation to the English Crown in the future.

A century later, when Edward I came to the throne in England, Alexander III made a trip south to give homage for his various properties in England. Edward made a rather half-hearted attempt to have Scotland included in the homage ceremony, but this was robustly rejected by Alexander, who told him that the Kingdom of Scotland was held 'from God alone', which Edward accepted – and there the matter rested.

Relations between the two countries were largely based on social relationships. Cross-border landholding was fairly commonplace, but although a Scottish lord might own several properties in England (or in France or Ireland) or vice versa, there was nobody who was a top-ranking noble (or magnate) in both kingdoms.

Naturally, any level of landholding automatically meant a degree of obligation to the Crown, and therefore anyone who held land in both countries had a range of responsibilities to both kings, but this had never been a serious problem before the English invasion of 1296, and its significance thereafter has been rather exaggerated by historians. The number of individuals involved was not terribly large in either kingdom and the properties concerned were mostly quite modest. No individual held a property of greater significance than a barony in more than one kingdom. Contrary to the claims of many writers in the past, neither Robert the Bruce nor John Comyn, nor even Alexander III, was considered a magnate in the English political structure, though all three of them did hold valuable English properties.

There was surprisingly little economic activity between the two countries. England's trade lay mainly with France, while Scotland's was with the Baltic and the Low Countries – the Netherlands and Belgium. Both countries depended on wool as the chief export and there was therefore little point in exporting wool from one to the other.

There was, however, a considerable degree of cultural overlap. Both kingdoms had adopted the political and military ethos of France that we now call feudalism. In England, this had come about through the Norman Conquest of 1066; in Scotland, it had occurred through a mixture of exposure to the practices of her southern neighbour, a considerable degree of intermarriage between the two royal families and the senior nobility, and the general adoption of feudal practice across northern and western Europe. In short, that was how a 'modern' nation functioned in the later Middle Ages.

Long before the outbreak of the Wars of Independence, there was precious little practical cultural, military or political difference between Scotland and England. There were some very clear regional differences within both countries, but little or nothing to distinguish the social ethos of Brechin from that of Bedford, save that the average 'parish gentry' landholder in Bedford might be more likely to speak French (or at least, be able to if they chose to do so) than his northern counterpart.

A PARTING OF THE WAYS

The generally cordial relationship between England and Scotland started to unravel with the death of Alexander III in March 1286. Alexander's two sons by his first marriage had already died, and his granddaughter, Margaret ('Maid of Norway', daughter of Erik II of Norway), had been recognised as his heir at the age of 3. There is a possibility that Alexander and Edward were planning a dynastic union of the two countries, which would be achieved by the marriage of Margaret to Edward's eldest son – the future Edward II – but Alexander was still only in his forties, and had married Yolande de Dreux in 1285, clearly hoping to produce a direct heir.

Alexander's death did not cause an immediate crisis. The Scottish political community was supportive, although the prospect of a female heir, especially one who was still a child, was certainly an unusual thing in medieval Europe. The political situation did, however, become a major issue when Margaret died en route to Scotland in 1290.

There were now two serious claimants to the throne, John Balliol and Robert Bruce (grandfather of the man who would become Robert I), and a number of others who might make claims of more dubious validity. Since the death of Alexander, Scotland had been administered by a council of 'guardians' representing the major political groups in the community. This system had worked well for the intervening four years, but the question of the succession was too momentous to be decided by a council of lords and clerics, and there was no prospect of reaching a unanimous agreement, since the council contained supporters of both of the significant candidates.

The council approached Edward I for advice. They have attracted a great deal of criticism from historians over the years for bringing Edward

into the discussions at all, but their actions were perfectly rational. Edward had had a good relationship with the late Alexander III; he was known to have a real interest in jurisprudence; he was powerful enough to impose the final decision if necessary; and he was acceptable to both of the main contenders. As the King of Scotland's only neighbour and a major player on the European political stage, he simply could not be ignored, and if the process degenerated into a civil war – and that was a real possibility – Edward might well allow the two sides to exhaust themselves and simply march into Scotland at the head of a great army and take over, as he had in Wales.

Edward was more than happy to take on the role, correctly identifying it as an opportunity to further his own interests in Scotland. The council did everything they reasonably could to ensure the future security of the realm, but Edward was an astute politician and would clearly have had a strong negotiating position. He was not invited to arbitrate on the question of the succession – his role was to conduct a court of enquiry, ensure a fair and equitable process and then oversee the installation of the successful candidate.

In due course, a grand jury of 104 auditors was assembled. The auditors include forty chosen by John Balliol and forty chosen by Robert Bruce, a clear indication that none of the other candidates really had a serious case to present, but were simply making a demonstration of their interest in the event that both the Bruce and Balliol lines might fail to produce heirs at some point in the future.

Edward was able to manipulate all of the candidates into accepting his overlordship as a condition of having their bids for the crown recognised at all. There was some resistance to this from various barons, but their position was undermined by the acceptance of Edward's demands by the different candidates.

The case ran for over a year, but in November a decision was finally reached, and John Balliol became King of Scotland, although he was obliged to give homage for his realm to Edward. Almost immediately, Edward's actions became increasingly overbearing. He asserted his right to hear appeals against John's Court judgements and generally set about undermining John's authority at every opportunity.

John was not in a position to challenge Edward's action, and his political credibility suffered accordingly. Edward hoped to provoke John into open resistance and the opportunity arose when Edward issued writs demanding military service from John and various prominent members of the Scottish nobility for service against France.

At around this time, the majority of the Scottish political community had taken power out of King John's hands. Initiatives of this nature were – to say the least – rare in medieval politics, but the process was eased by the fact that a committee of guardians had ruled effectively during the years between the death of Alexander III and the death of his granddaughter Margaret, a period of four years. The Scottish political community had acquired some experience of governing a kingdom without actually having a king – experience that would prove invaluable in the years between 1297 and 1304.

The new council made a treaty of mutual defence with the King of France, and from 1295 there was, in theory at least, a state of war between England and Scotland. In practice, however, very little happened. Edward was already busy with his war in France and was unable to pursue operations in Scotland until the spring of 1296. Both sides raised armies, but the Scots simply had no idea about how to conduct a war. There had not been war in Scotland for more than thirty years, and that had been a relatively short affair that had been dealt with by the county communities of the south-west.

Edward, on the other hand, was an experienced commander who pursued his campaign with purpose. The Scots made some rather ineffective raids into northern England, but Edward approached the town of Berwick in April 1296, stormed it, and sacked the community with enormous loss of life. The town – in those days, one of the most significant commercial centres in the British Isles – was largely destroyed, but Edward had effectively sent a signal to every other town in Scotland that resistance was not only futile, since hardly any Scottish towns had defences of any kind, let alone serious fortification, but would also result in the utter destruction of the community.

There was only one action in the rest of the 1296 campaign, when a body of Scottish men-at-arms encountered a similar English force near Dunbar and were completely routed. The term 'man-at-arms' did not just mean any soldier; it was specifically a fully armoured cavalryman with a good quality warhorse, also known as *armati* or *homines ad arma* (or 'armed men'). The term 'armed' meant armoured from head to toe, not 'armed' in our modern sense of carrying a weapon. These troops were the basic tool of day-to-day warfare and generally served a number of days per year as part of the rent of their property. This was called 'knight service', although only a tiny proportion of them were actually knights.

Only one fatality is recorded from the skirmish at Dunbar, but in the aftermath of the fighting and the subsequent surrender of Dunbar Castle, more than 200 members of the Scottish nobility and gentry were taken prisoner. The main body of the Scottish Army, now bereft of leadership and purpose, simply dissolved and made their way home without ever seeing action.

THE SCOTS REGROUP

King John's government had not enjoyed the full support of the political community. A certain Robert Bruce ('The Bruce', grandson of the man who had sought to become king in 1291–92) had sided with Edward I in the hope that his father (his grandfather had died in the interim) would now be installed on the throne at the hands of Edward I.

He was quickly disabused of this; Edward had no plans to make anybody King of Scotland.

Instead, Edward marched northwards demanding homage and the surrender of castles and towns – all of which were easily accomplished given the events at Berwick. By July, he had captured King John, forced his abdication and packed him off to London as a prisoner. Assuming – perhaps understandably – that the war was won, Edward left the consolidation of his occupation government to his lieutenants and returned to the more pressing affairs at home.

The Scots had certainly been defeated and Edward had obliged a great number of Scottish nobles and towns to give homage, but their recovery was rapid. Within a matter of months, Edward's officers reported that the Scots were in the process of forming a government and were appointing officials in many areas. Only two counties – Berwickshire and Roxburgh – were properly under English control, and they 'only lately'.

Any hopes that Edward had of imposing his own rule quickly and securely disappeared in early 1297. One of the prisoners taken the previous year, Sir Andrew Murray, escaped from captivity, made his way back to the north-east of Scotland and raised a force which set siege to strongholds. Robert Bruce had decided to jump ship and was assembling a force at Irvine with a number of other lords, in what we now call the 'Noble Revolt', while William Wallace, youngest son of an obscure Ayrshire knight, was conducting operations in central Scotland.

Bruce was now fighting for King John, although he had been conspicuous by his absence the previous year. His enthusiasm for the Balliol cause was purely a matter of long-term self-interest. In practice, if he ever wanted to be king himself, Bruce had to be seen to be espousing the cause of independence, and in 1297 that meant supporting John. More to the point, if John was to return to power, Bruce would have to have a very good story to tell to avoid being forfeited and exiled – if not executed – for his failure to fight for the Balliol cause in the past.

The prospect of King John being restored to authority was not as unlikely as it might seem. He had been deposed at sword point, but not at the cost of a destructive campaign with heavy casualties; armies could still be raised and his fortunes could be turned by military means. Equally, it was not impossible that Edward I might choose to reverse John's forfeiture. Earls and lords who forfeited their power after rebellion in times of civil war were quite often later restored to their estates. Even if they were not restored themselves, it was not uncommon for their heirs to be reinstated, and John Balliol had a son. Edward I was intermittently at war in relation to his lordships in France and the King of France had some degree of sympathy for John and Scotland as a potential ally against Edward's aggression. It was not impossible that the price of some future peace treaty, or even just a long truce, might result in John's return.

The situation was complex and fraught with danger for Robert Bruce, but for his own allies at Irvine, and for Wallace and Murray, the matter was more clear-cut. They were simply fighting to get John restored to the throne.

The Battle of Stirling Bridge, September 1297

Due to his commitments elsewhere, Edward was unable to take to the field himself and entrusted operations in Scotland to his lieutenants. The Noble Revolt by Bruce and others was resolved through negotiations at Irvine, although there was a strong suspicion that he dragged the discussions out as long as he could to allow Wallace and Murray more time to gather and train their troops. True or not, by the time that Sir Hugh Cressingham – Edward's Treasurer for Scotland – was able to get to Stirling, he found that Murray and Wallace had combined their forces on the north bank of the river. Confident that his force was more than a match for anything the Scots might have to offer, Cressingham tried to cross the river and was soundly defeated.

Wallace & Murray Take Control

Wallace and Murray were now effectively masters of Scotland north of the River Forth and throughout much of the south. They took the role of joint Guardians of the Realm (regents) in the name of King John, but Murray died a few weeks after the battle – possibly of wounds incurred in the action – leaving Wallace in sole charge. It was rare indeed for someone of such lowly political status to acquire so much power, but there was something of a political vacuum at the time. Some of the more prominent lords had already been neutralised at Irvine; some simply wanted a quiet life and were prepared to accept Edward's lordship; while others – particularly in the south-east, where they were most vulnerable to English military power – were hesitant to resist or had English garrisons in their castles; but most significantly, a large number were still prisoners of war following the debacle of the 1296 campaign.

At about this time, Edward freed a number of senior figures – notably Sir John Comyn, Lord of Badenoch – to serve in his army in Flanders in exchange for their liberty, only to have them defect and escape to France at the earliest opportunity and then return to Scotland to continue the fight. Clearly, he had to act if he was to achieve his goals in Scotland, but he was unable to bring an army to the field until the late summer of 1298.

The Battle of Falkirk, July 1298

By this time, most of Scotland was under Wallace's control, and initially Edward struggled to come to grips with his opponent. Just as he was on the verge of running out of money and supplies, Edward was able to steal a march on Wallace and inflicted a major defeat on him at Falkirk. Since Wallace's political authority had depended entirely on his military credibility, he was swiftly ousted from the position of Guardian and his place was taken by Bruce and Comyn.

This was not a happy arrangement. The Comyns had an excellent track record as servants of the Crown and were closely associated with King John, but Bruce had been on the English side in 1296 and clearly had royal ambitions of his own. All things considered, Comyn and Bruce managed their campaign reasonably effectively for some time, but it was always tense at best and seriously hostile at worst.

THE STRATHORD AGREEMENT, 1304

In the aftermath of Falkirk, Edward was obliged to leave Scotland once again to tend to concerns elsewhere and may even have believed that the Scottish situation was now largely settled and could be left to his subordinates. This was clearly not the case. In 1299 – at the behest of the Pope and as part of negotiations with France – Edward released John Balliol, and by 1300 there seemed to be a real possibility that he might be restored to the throne. This was not an attractive proposition to Robert Bruce, who now made his peace with Edward, abandoning the Balliol cause. The terms of Bruce's return to Edward's peace are – perhaps deliberately – rather vague, and it may be that Edward held out the possibility that Robert might, in the future, be granted the Scottish throne, doubtless on the same basis as it had been held by John.

It was not uncommon for kings to owe allegiance to other kings. Edward himself owed allegiance to the King of France for his lordships there, and Alexander III had owed allegiance to Edward for a number of estates in England – though not for his kingdom. Owing allegiance for a kingdom was rare, but not unknown, and from Bruce's point of view, holding a kingdom by the permission of Edward would have been a good deal more attractive than being driven out of his earldom and lordships by John.

Despite Bruce's defection, the Scots continued to make headway, but remained a long way from victory. They were able to acquire control over much of the country, but the network of strong castles in the south and east was a very hard nut to crack. On the other hand, Edward could not make an opportunity to take matters into his own hands until he had reached a satisfactory conclusion in France. He was making little progress, until the French were badly defeated by the people of Flanders at the Battle of Courtrai in July 1302. This put Edward in a position of strength – or at least, Philip IV was in a position of temporary weakness – and he was able to force a peace treaty which specifically excluded the Scots and secured a statement in which King John rejected any further involvement in Scottish affairs.

The loss of France as an ally was a body blow to the Scots. Philip IV's refusal to negotiate a peace with Edward unless it included a political settlement for Scotland had been a crucial part of Scotland's diplomatic campaign. Worse still, since John was no longer interested in his own restoration, it was now difficult for his supporters to really be clear about what they were fighting for. Additionally, Edward now brought a large army to Scotland, but at the same time made it clear that he was prepared to negotiate terms.

In February 1304, an agreement was reached at Strathord and the war came to an end. For Edward, this was a very important achievement. Aware that he was nearing the end of his life, he was eager to finish his Scottish business. But it is not at all clear that he really believed he had secured his authority; at least a proportion of the Scots seem to have seen the Strathord Agreement as more of an armistice than a final settlement, and a few prominent figures – notably William Wallace – were specifically excluded from the terms and were thus still active in the field.

THE EXECUTION OF WILLIAM WALLACE, 1305

The exclusion of Wallace and a few others from the Strathord Agreement was, to some extent, a matter of public relations. The garrison of Stirling Castle – which had also been specifically excluded from the Strathord terms – had held out for some time, declaring that they were not fighting for Balliol's kingship, but for 'the Lion' (the heraldic symbol of the nation). However, with no prospect of relief, their resistance was probably more to do with seeking honourable terms than anything else.

Wallace was a different matter. The Scottish war had been a heavy burden on Edward's kingdom and someone had to carry the can and satisfy English public opinion. Edward issued a bounty for his capture and in August 1305, Wallace was captured near Glasgow and taken to London, where he was subjected to a travesty of a trial and executed.

Overall, the execution of Wallace – and the manner of it – was an unwise move on the part of Edward. Wallace was, by this time, politically insignificant, but deliberate persecution made Edward look petty and the elaborate executions were not part of the general ethos of medieval Scotland. Had Edward simply imprisoned him, Wallace would probably have fallen out of public consciousness along with the other men who had resisted the occupation and are now known only to a handful of medieval scholars and enthusiasts.

Although he felt the need to make an example, and perhaps demonstrate a degree of 'closure' to his Scottish wars, Edward could not afford to impose too heavy a settlement on the Scottish magnates and the wider political community. If he was to rule successfully, he needed their support to run the country. It was clear that he could not simply execute all of the nobles who had fought against him and replace them with English lords – there were not enough candidates, and such a policy would inevitably breed hostility. Moreover, he could not possibly execute all the sons, cousins and nephews of Scottish lords who might, at some point, rebel in order to try to recover their lost heritages and would be able to gather support from the community quite easily.

Edward had not made sweeping changes to administrative or legal practices in Scotland. The only law he abolished was the 'law of the Scots and the Brets', which, in practice, had actually been out of use for generations. But his occupation government was seen as oppressive and – inevitably – foreign. It is important to remember that in the Middle Ages, England and Scotland were as much different countries as Portugal and France. This may have genuinely been rather lost on Edward himself, since there was a good deal of common practice in both kingdoms.

His general intention toward Scotland is less than clear. He made no effort to formally incorporate Scotland into England, nor did he arrange to have himself formally declared as king. It is possible that he hoped to achieve a situation where Scotland would be a kind of independent stand-alone lordship, owned by the English Crown but not subject to interference by the English Parliament. He seems to have had no intention of ever calling a Scottish Parliament. Instead, he set up a council of magnates – mostly Scottish – and entrusted administration to them.

Edward may have genuinely believed that the death of Wallace was the final act in the conquest of Scotland, although that would have been a rather optimistic assessment. There were at least two possible sources of contention. One was Robert Bruce, who was certainly in Edward's peace, but is most unlikely to have given up on his regal ambitions at any point. The other was Edward Balliol, son of the deposed King John.

John's deposition and abdication had been forced at the point of the sword and was therefore easily recognisable as an act of coercion by a greater military power. Medieval legal practice understood the concept of duress and John's abdication was thus invalid in itself. In 1303 he had surrendered all his rights in Scottish matters, but it was questionable as to whether he could legally discard the claims of his heir. Edward Balliol was still young and, in due course, might well attempt to restore the family line. The Scottish political establishment was rather conservative and if Edward Balliol could bring any sort of a force to Scotland, there was every chance that he would be able to gather widespread support since he was, after all, the legitimate heir to the throne.

2

KING ROBERT'S WAR

Through the autumn and winter of 1305/06 there seems to have been no serious opposition to Edward's rule in Scotland. The royal castles – and some baronial ones – were garrisoned, and work continued on the construction of a number of 'peels', though not with any great sense of urgency. The garrisons were mostly quite small and, all in all, there was a brief period of peace; but the situation was far from settled. Robert Bruce was still determined to acquire the throne and in February 1306 he met with his chief political rival, John Comyn.

According to John Barbour, Archdeacon of Aberdeen, in his 1375 poem *The Bruce*, Robert Bruce offered to grant all of his property – most significantly the Earldom of Carrick and the Lordship of Annandale – to Comyn in exchange for unequivocal support for Bruce's kingship. Alternatively, Bruce would give his support to Comyn in exchange for all of the great Comyn lordships of the northeast. Barbour's account is – at best – suspect in this regard. The Bruce claim to the throne was weaker than that of the Balliols, but he would certainly be the next legitimate heir to the throne if the Balliol line was excluded or died out. Any claim for the Comyn family, however, would have been tenuous in the extreme, unless the entire Balliol and Bruce families were to die out.

Regardless, the two men met at Greyfriars Church, in Dumfries, on 10 February 1306 for some purpose; a meeting that resulted in the death of John Comyn. The full story of events that day is much debated by historians. It is not known whether Comyn's death was intentional or an accident. It is almost certain that Bruce and Comyn were planning to take action against the occupation. The Comyns' long tradition of loyal service to the Crown would suggest that John Comyn favoured a coup that would, in due course, put Edward Balliol on the throne, but that might be a threat to the Bruce family since they had not supported John's kingship in 1296 and had only fought for him intermittently thereafter.

The murder – or, at best, manslaughter – of John Comyn may have propelled Robert forward, in a bid for the crown, sooner than he would have wished, but the speed with which his supporters responded was remarkable and it would seem likely that his plans were already quite advanced. The town of Ayr was seized for Robert by Sir Reginald Crawford and Sir Bryce Blair in February, along with several other strongholds – Dumfries, Tibbers and Dalswinton, among others. However, the English recovered Ayr shortly afterwards and Blair and Crawford were captured and executed. They had made some effort to damage the castle, but not, it would seem, very effectively, since it was repaired quickly and at negligible cost later in the year.

The Bruce supporters' activity was not limited to seizing towns and castles. An English record refers to chargers (warhorses) being lost in action at Nithsdale on 18 March, which indicates an engagement with the Scots, but there seems to be no further information. The absence of the names of leaders or casualties would suggest that this was a very small action and absolutely typical of the normal practice of war at the time. Barbour's omission of the fight at Nithsdale from his lengthy litany of battles suggests perhaps that the Scots fared badly; however, the sheer volume of actions during this period may have allowed this one to slip past Barbour – and, indeed, the other chroniclers, both English and Scottish.

Although Robert's forces were able to make rapid progress in the south-west, his forces were slender and his hold on the region was shaky. As Earl of Carrick and Lord of Annandale his influence was considerable, and of course he would call out his tenants to discharge their military obligations, but he could not keep them in the field for very long without the resources to feed them, and, in the case of the infantry, they had to get back to their farms.

Equally, Edward I was not in a position to mount an immediate counter-offensive on any scale.

It would take some time to raise the money and arrange recruitment for a powerful force. Following the agreement at Strathord, he had reduced the strength of most of his garrisons across Scotland on the assumption that Scottish landholders who owed knight service would fill the ranks as required. This had been reasonably effective over the previous year and more – Wallace had been captured by just such a force led by a Scottish knight fulfilling his duty to keep the peace. On the other hand, Wallace had no more than a handful of companions in 1305 and had been reduced to little more than a bandit; it was not at all clear that he could count on any support in the community, other than by the threat of the sword.

Bruce was a different proposition. He was a great lord in his own right and might well be able to procure some powerful allies. There was every chance that he would be able to raise a force that was too much for the garrisons to deal with. In any case, the purpose of the garrisons was to protect Edward's administration. If he were to strip them of men it could invite a wider insurgency – one that would endanger the network of castles on which the occupation depended.

Initially, Edward I seems to have been in some doubt about whether Robert was actually starting an insurrection at all. This was not an unreasonable doubt, given that Robert had now been in Edward's allegiance for some time, was married to the daughter of one of Edward's most loyal lieutenants, and had only recently paid homage to Edward for the English estates that he had inherited from his father. Moreover, as Sheriff of Ayr, Robert was a senior officer in Edward's occupation government.

There is little doubt that Robert Bruce had his sights set on the Scottish throne throughout his adult life, but the declaration of his kingship was forced on him before his plans had matured. He would probably have preferred to wait until the death of Edward I before making his move, but the murder of Sir John Comyn forced him to claim the crown immediately or face conventional criminal proceedings for murder.

THE BRUCE TAKES ACTION

By late March, Edward had received reliable information that Robert had indeed made his move and he now appointed Aymer de Valence to act as his military lieutenant. De Valence was to take the place of John of Brittany, who had been Edward's chief lieutenant in Scotland since 1305. The new appointee was given wide-ranging powers to demand military service from Scots who were in Edward's peace and to forfeit and execute those who joined Bruce.

Initially, that power was to be applied to all captives as a summary sentence; however, Edward stepped back from that for a number of reasons. First, he wanted to ensure that any high-profile captives could be taken to London to be executed in the kind of gory, gaudy ritual that had been suffered by William Wallace. Edward believed – quite correctly, in all probability – that public executions were good for his standing with the London mob. More importantly, perhaps, mandatory executions would inevitably tie the hands of de Valence and make it very difficult – in fact, impossible – to persuade people to defect from the Bruce camp.

Bruce's hastily arranged coronation was accompanied by attempts to gather support, especially among the senior nobility. Given that the Scottish political community as a whole had accepted terms from Edward I only two years before and that the new king was something of an unknown quantity, in addition to being both a usurper and possibly a sacrilegious murderer, it is hardly surprising that the Scottish political establishment did not flock to his banner in droves. In addition to that, Robert had already changed sides more than once.

In 1295–96, he had refused to support King John and had served in Edward's army. In 1297, he had defected to the Balliol cause for the duration of the short-lived Noble Revolt, before making terms with

Edward. He had returned to the Balliol cause after the defeat of Wallace, but returned to Edward's allegiance long before the Strathord Agreement of 1304. Taking up arms in the cause of someone with such a track record of inconstancy – whatever the reason – was hardly an attractive prospect. If Robert won – and that must have looked very questionable – then all would be well. If he lost, the possibility of being hanged was a very real one. If, as might be possible given the twists and turns of previous years, Robert made terms with Edward, those who had joined his cause would very probably be pardoned, but at what cost? And what would his supporters have gained for their risk?

Despite a stream of modest successes in March and April, Bruce was already suffering setbacks by early summer. Two of his most important supporters, the Bishops of Glasgow and St Andrews, had been quickly taken out of the struggle.

The support of the clergy was a crucial prop to the kingship of Robert I. The Bishop of Glasgow, Robert Wishart, joined the Bruce cause immediately after Robert's assumption of kingship. The bishop had been granted timber for the renovation of the bell tower of Glasgow Cathedral by Edward I, but used it for the construction of siege equipment to reduce Kirkintilloch Castle in the spring or early summer of 1306.

Bishop Lamberton of St Andrews claimed to have been forced into giving his allegiance to the Bruce cause in the summer of 1306, but only after he had called out his tenants to serve in Robert's army. In the far north of Scotland, where English armies seldom penetrated and never lingered long, the Bishop of Ross told his diocese that it was just as spiritually valuable to fight against the occupation as it was to go on a Crusade to the Holy Land: either would be a fight against 'God's Foes'.

The loss of the Bishops of Glasgow and St Andrews was quite a blow to Robert's campaign. Both men were able diplomats and shrewd advisers, but they also had control over a great deal of wealth. St Andrews was one of the richest dioceses in the British Isles and Robert would have been glad of its financial support.

THE BATTLE OF METHVEN

Despite these setbacks, Robert was able to recruit a modest army and establish himself at his camp in a wood to the south of the River Almond near Methven, close to the town of Perth, on or around 18 June 1306. The town had been occupied by Aymer de Valence, and before sunrise the next day, while many of Robert's troops were absent in billets or on foraging missions, de Valence assembled his troops and made a surprise attack on the Scots. There was a brief, fierce engagement, but the Scots were heavily outclassed and outnumbered.

According to Barbour, the English force was the stronger by about 1,500 men. However, the *The Chronicle of Walter of Guisborough* puts de Valence's command at 300 men-at-arms and a contingent of infantry. This may be a literary device, however, rather than realistic estimate of the force. Robert's recruiting campaigns may not have been terribly successful, but given that more than 100 landholders had declared for the Bruce cause, it is likely that King Robert had a force of men-at-arms at his disposal of rather more than 300 and that de Valence's force was numerically inferior.

On the other hand, de Valence was a very experienced commander and his troops were concentrated in the town rather than scattered about the countryside. Clearly, he identified a favourable opportunity and struck hard. Within a short period, the Scots were routed and Robert was obliged to leave the area with only a few hundred followers, taking to the hills to avoid pursuit.

The Guisborough account throws an interesting sidelight on the confidence – or lack of it – of those Scottish nobles who had joined the Bruce cause. The chronicle claims that the Scottish men-at-arms covered their arms (that is, their heraldic devices) with white sheets. As Professor A.A.M. Duncan has observed, this can only have been done as a means of avoiding identification should the battle go badly. It is less than likely that the Scots knights and men-at-arms would have been aware of Edward's intention to hang any captives, so identification in that sense was probably not uppermost in their minds. In fact, they would be more likely to assume that if they were captured they would be ransomed. However, a man with no device clearly displayed would be unlikely to be seen as a candidate for ransom and therefore more likely to be killed out of hand. More to the point, de Valence's attack very clearly took the Scots by surprise and it seems improbable that the men in question would have taken the time to cover their shields.

The battle was brief and nearly went very badly indeed for the Scots. Sir Philip Moubray, a Scot with English allegiance, almost captured Robert, but was prevented from doing so by Sir Christopher Seton, an English knight in Bruce's service. The defeat was serious, but not completely crushing. King Robert was able to extricate a force of a few hundred and make his escape; the question was, what should they do next?

THE BATTLE OF DALRY

After his defeat at the Battle of Methven, Robert
headed toward Atholl with a small following – 300
men, according to Barbour – only to be confronted
at Dalry, a hamlet near Tyndrum, by a force raised
predominantly from the MacDougall family, one of
the most powerful groupings in western Scotland
and close allies of the Comyn family. The chronicler, John of Fordoun, dated the engagement to
14 August 1306 and located the battle further west,
on the border of Atholl and Argyll, but it seems
likely that the action took place rather earlier with
Bruce being driven away from Perth by de Valence.
Who exactly Robert was fighting cannot be established from Barbour's account, but he refers to the
'Lord of Lorne' and the Barons of Argyll, and puts
their strength at 1,000 men – a credible number.

Bruce's army suffered some casualties and he lost
several (or possibly all) of his remaining precious
heavy cavalry horses, but he was able to extricate
some of his men and escape from the field. With his
army reduced to a mere handful of men, Robert was
obliged to send his queen and family north to seek
safety in the north-east while he and his remaining
followers took to the hills.

Tradition has it that he left Scotland and spent
some months on the island of Rathlin off the

northern coast of Ireland. If so, he would have been vulnerable to the sea power of Edward, who certainly ordered ships to the west coast to search for Robert's party. It is difficult to see how Rathlin would have been able to support even a very small body of men without help from outside; however, it is possible that Edward's forces failed to reach Rathlin and Bruce's party may have been able to feed themselves by force of arms.

DAUNTING NEWS

Unsurprisingly, while Robert was hiding out, his cause did not prosper. The various strongholds that had been seized in his name, and those belonging to his family and allies, were quickly captured or recovered. Loch Doon Castle was taken by an English force under Sir Henry Percy, sometime between August and October. Robert had entrusted the castle to one of his closest associates, Sir Christopher Seton. A later charter of Robert I tells us that the castle was betrayed by one Arthur, a nephew of Sir Gilbert Carrick. Seton was captured and executed at Dumfries; a sign of Edward's policy and of things to come.

There was worse news for Robert from the north-east. His brother Nigel was taken prisoner at Kildrummy Castle after a short siege in August – the grain supply having been set alight by a saboteur named Osbern. Worse yet, his wife and daughter, his sister and the Countess of Buchan had been taken prisoner by the Earl of Ross, who ignored the right of sanctuary they claimed in the Chapel of St Duthach at Tain.

Nigel Bruce was taken to London for one of Edward's barbarous execution rituals and the female prisoners were sent into solitary confinement. The Countess of Buchan and Mary Bruce (Robert's sister) were held in cages on public display at Roxburgh and Berwick castles. Elizabeth de Burgh (Robert's wife) could not be treated quite so harshly, since her father was the Earl of Ulster and an important figure in Edward's government, but she was still put into solitary confinement save for two servant women who were to be 'elderly and not at all gay'.

The last of the female prisoners – Robert's daughter, Marjorie Bruce, who was about 12 years of age – was put in a cage as well. Hers was to be at the Tower of London and she was to be allowed to speak with no one apart from the constable in command of the castle. Uncharacteristically, Edward relented and decided that she would be imprisoned in a convent instead.

Quite what Edward hoped to achieve by these horrific acts is hard to say. They may have helped to dissuade people from supporting the Bruce cause, but they can hardly have done anything to persuade them that he was a humane or honourable person.

WHEREABOUTS UNKNOWN

There is no way of knowing when Robert became aware of what had befallen his family and friends, but by September 1306 he was at the castle of Dunaverty, then he simply disappeared. He may have spent time at Rathlin, or in other parts of northern and eastern Ireland – he had, or at least had claim to, various lordships there and undoubtedly had friends that he could turn to. He may have made his way to the Hebrides or to the Northern Isles – Orkney and Shetland – or even to Norway, where his sister was the dowager queen.

Wherever he went, Bruce avoided leaving any trace for historians until late January or early February 1307. According to the Guisborough chronicle, he sent agents to collect rents from his tenants at the end of September (though Scottish rents were generally paid at Martinmas, 11 November) which has a ring of credibility, given that he must have been very short of money.

In February, two of Robert's brothers, Alexander (Dean of Glasgow) and Thomas, in company with Sir Reginald Crawford and Malcolm MacQuillan, Lord of Kintyre, arrived in Galloway with a substantial force of eighteen ships, only to be defeated and captured by Dungal MacDouall. MacDouall executed MacQuillan there and then, and packed the Bruce brothers off to London, where they too suffered death in one of Edward's hideous execution processes.

Another group, under James Douglas and Sir Robert Boyd, led a raid on Arran. They took a galley to the island and ambushed a ration party taking stores to Brodick Castle. The garrison heard the clash of arms and a party of men-at-arms was dispatched to rescue the ration party. However, Douglas and Boyd's force was the stronger and drove the garrison troops back to the castle.

TURNBERRY, FEBRUARY 1307

Although little is known of Robert's movements in this period, Barbour's assertion that he was in Arran for some time immediately prior to his return to the mainland is a realistic proposition, although that may not have been for more than a matter of days. He certainly seems to have been there with such troops as he had to hand when he made his next move.

An arrangement had been made for an agent scout to set a fire not far from the Bruce family stronghold of Turnberry Castle if the prospects looked promising for a raid. The agent thought not, and so did not light his fire, but, by chance, another fire nearby was seen from Arran and Bruce mistakenly led his party across the water.

The castle was in the hands of the Northumberland Lord Sir Henry Percy and was a crucial part of Edward I's occupation government in the region. The garrison became aware that something was going on and, with the walls manned, the castle was too tough a nut for Robert's force. Instead, they turned their attention to the village of Turnberry, where they killed a number of Percy's troops, who presumably had been billeted there.

EVADING CAPTURE

Over the next few months, Robert seems to have led a very mobile life. According to Barbour, he was leading the English a merry dance, but a more likely interpretation would be that he was being pursued around the country whenever Edward's government could locate him and raise enough troops to try to bring him to battle.

The difficulty of communication meant that achieving both of these things at the same time was more of a problem than we might expect. Edward maintained quite a lot of troops in Scotland and he could count on support from various Scottish magnates, but he could not possibly afford the manpower or money to keep a substantial army in the field indefinitely and still keep garrisons in every town and castle. His officers might be able to ascertain Bruce's location at a given moment, but that was of little value if they could not bring an adequate enough force to be confident of victory.

However much Barbour dwells on tales of Robert being alone in the hills, he clearly had more men under arms than just a handful of close companions. He was undoubtedly able to recruit from his own estates in the south-west, but he had to have started his 1307 campaign with a body of troops worthy of the name and they must surely have been recruited in the West Highlands and Hebrides from the lands of his connections and relations. He certainly enjoyed the support of Christian MacRuarie and Angus Og – major landholders with castles, ships and soldiers that they could lend to the Bruce cause.

The fact that many western lords were unhappy at the prospect of John of Lorn using Edward's patronage to become an ever-greater power on the western seaboard may not have done Robert any harm either.

RAIDS AND AMBUSHES

The new campaign would not be marked by the raising of great armies and the application of grand manoeuvres, but of minor raids and ambushes calculated to undermine the confidence of Plantagenet garrisons and the local landholders and communities in the value of those garrisons. If the garrisons could not protect themselves, how were they going to be able to protect the farms and businesses on which the community depended?

Edward was well aware of Bruce's activities, and less than happy with the efforts being made by his own supporters. As early as the middle of February, he was already sending angry messages to his chief lieutenant, Aymer de Valence, and demanding firm and fast action. De Valence set about the business of cornering Robert with every hope and expectation of inflicting another defeat, hopefully a fatal one. He found Bruce's force at Glentrool, but failed to achieve surprise. A short and sharp battle ensued and although de Valence's losses were not very heavy, he certainly had the worst of the encounter and beat a hasty retreat.

It is misleading to characterise Robert's early campaigns as 'guerrilla' warfare; the activities and engagements were very much in the general style of medieval warfare. Great battles were exceptionally rare, even when large armies had been raised with the specific intention of ensuring that there would be a general engagement. The size of a battle is also seldom a useful guide to its significance. Robert's force at this time was certainly no more than a few hundred, and although Barbour tells us that de Valence had an army of thousands, we can be confident that this was not the case. Barbour's agenda was, naturally, to do everything he could to enhance the reputation of his hero, Robert the Bruce. However, an English force of any great magnitude would likely have left rather more evidence in the form of Crown records. Wage rolls, supply demands and the compensation (or *restauro*) for lost warhorses were part of the normal conditions of service for English knights and men-at-arms – or for Scottish ones in English service.

The latter were an important part of Edward's military establishment. All the landholders who had come to Edward's peace owed whatever military service was due from their estates. Failure to turn out as required could lead to forfeiture and Edward was hardly in a forgiving frame of mind. However, it is far too easy to dismiss the Scotsmen who served Edward as being traitors to their country. Some of them had accepted his terms in 1296 or 1304 and felt bound by their word but, in any case, why should they do anything to help Robert Bruce? He was most certainly not the legitimate king. John Balliol's abdication had been made at sword point and was therefore – at best – of questionable validity. Even if it had been a voluntary action, his son Edward should be the rightful king, not Robert Bruce. Additionally, Robert was not only at war with Edward, he was at war with the Comyn family and all their allies.

The fight at Glentrool was not large, but neither was it insignificant. Barbour concludes his account with the information that there was a lot of ill feeling in the English Army about the fact that they had been defeated by such a slender force and this resulted in a fight between a prominent English knight, Sir Robert Clifford, and Sir John de Vaus (or Vaux). Sir John may have been the Northumberland knight of that name who served in a variety of administrative and military roles in the Scottish Government of Edward I, but he may equally have been the Lord of Dirleton, a small, wealthy barony in East Lothian. It may be that this fight was just an indication of nationality tensions in the ranks of the English Army. The portion of the Scottish political community (including the Lord of Dirleton) who had supported King John had come to terms with Edward I at Strathord as recently as February 1304, after eight years of war. It would hardly be surprising if English soldiers had doubts about some of their new comrades in arms.

THE BATTLE OF LOUDOUN HILL, MAY 1307

A victory – even a small one – did Robert no harm, and by May he was conducting operations from Galston in Ayrshire, extorting support from the local populace, when he learned of the approach of an English force – once again commanded by Sir Aymer de Valence. Robert was aware that there was really only one route that de Valence could take if he was to catch the Scots, and was thus able to choose the battlefield with some care. What Barbour calls the 'hey gat' – the High Road – along which de Valence's force would have to march, lay between two morasses, each a bow shot (perhaps 200 yards) from the road.

The Scottish force would have been fairly small, some hundreds probably, and could not

hope to face up to de Valence's cavalry on a wide swath of hard ground, but it was desirable that Robert should get a more impressive victory than Glentrool under his belt if he were to retain the support of the men he had already enlisted, let alone recruit more. Additionally, de Valence's force was probably rather more mobile than that of the

Scottish King. If he did not fight at a place of his own choosing, then he might well have to fight on de Valence's terms.

The site he had selected was not sufficiently advantageous, as it stood, so Robert took measures to make the ground more suitable for his own force and more dangerous for his enemy. He had three trenches cut on either side of the road, each running at right angles to the morasses. The trenches and the piles of spoil cast up from them served to break up the battlefield in such a way that the English cavalry could not be deployed to their best advantage, and would be obliged to advance on the Scots on a very narrow front.

When the English Army came into view, the main body of the Scottish Army left the higher ground from which they had observed their approach and deployed for battle between the foremost of the three pairs of ditches, presumably with the intention of retiring to the next pair should the fight go badly. This seems to have been unnecessary. The English cavalry attacked the Scots, but could not outflank them on account of the ditches and could not break into the Scottish formation. The action was probably of very short duration; once it was clear that the Scots could not be shifted, there would have been no point in continuing the attack.

Barbour's account, naturally enough, makes Loudoun Hill a major battle, but it is clear from English records that it was a relatively minor affair in terms of the numbers involved. However, its significance was more to do with morale and confidence than strategic or tactical outcomes. It would be unrealistic to suggest that after Loudoun Hill, King Robert never looked back – he would have to deal with a variety of setbacks, but Loudoun did give him a victory that would lose nothing in the retelling. On a personal level, it must have been most satisfactory for Robert to have beaten the man who had defeated him in his first battle command, but the boost to the confidence of his army was a matter of the utmost importance.

Barbour's suggestion that the English Army included thousands of men-at-arms should not be taken at face value. All of the English garrisons in Scotland, including Scots in English service, would not have amounted to so many. However, since de Valence was actively seeking battle with King Robert, it is reasonable to assume that his force was a strong one. According to Barbour, the Scottish Army comprised 600 fighting men (only a few of whom – perhaps 10 per cent – would have been men-at-arms) and a similar number of non-combatants drawn up to their rear. Barbour states that Bruce drew up his troops in one body and the others in a second formation, possibly in the hope that from a distance they might be perceived as a combat unit. This might explain the failure of the English Army to press on as hard as they might otherwise have done in the belief that if they defeated the leading Scottish formation they would still have another to deal with, or that they might be outflanked once they were heavily engaged. The battle was not large, but it was not unimportant. It could not be dismissed as a mere skirmish or an unfortunate ambush. A major force had gone in search of battle, found it, and been roundly defeated.

Just a few days later, on or around 13 May, Bruce was able to defeat another force, this time a cavalry column under Gilbert de Clare, the Earl of Gloucester, who was obliged to beat a hasty retreat to Ayr Castle.

THE DEATH OF EDWARD I

Victories – even small ones – gave Robert prestige and undermined the credibility of the occupation government, but there was little Edward could do about it. He was not just ill, he was dying. When he eventually breathed his last, the Bruce cause was still weak, but it was rapidly gaining strength.

Two strands of evidence throw light on this, beyond the ebb and flow of purely military matters.

The Guisborough and Lanercost chroniclers tell us that feelings were so strong against the occupation that, despite the threat of the most horrible death penalties imaginable, people were prepared to take up arms for Bruce so that they would not be tried by English judges. One of Edward's Scottish supporters reported that if Bruce were to make his way into the north of Scotland he would have the 'people all ready at his will more entirely than ever'. He went on to tell of a local prophecy that, after the death of Edward, the Scots (and also the Welsh) would gain 'full lordship' – that is to say, political independence.

These are rather telling statements for a number of reasons. Edward's correspondent wrote to him on 15 May, just five days after de Valence's defeat at Glentrool and Gloucester's defeat, three days later. It is perfectly possible that he was unaware of either of those engagements. Even if he did know of them – and for the second fight especially that would seem less likely – they surely had not had time to really permeate the consciousness of the wider community. Either way, the officer concerned (Professor Barrow [2005] suggests it was Sir Alexander Abernethy, a long-standing member of Edward's administration) clearly felt that the people had already favoured Bruce in the past and were now more enthusiastic.

Quite why that should be the case is a challenge for modern views on medieval political history. If by 'the people' the writer meant the gentry and nobility, that is a something of a curiosity. The Bruce family had no great tradition of local lordship and influence outside the south-west, and the great lords of the north were the Comyns, who had always supported the Balliols until 1304 and then accepted Edward's sovereignty. On the other hand, if the writer means the wider community, that is just as odd. It is widely believed that nationalism is a modern political phenomenon that owes its genesis to the wars of Napoleon, yet here we see three contemporary writers alluding to some kind of nationalism as a motivation. Given the scarcity of recorded evidence that refers to public opinion at all – as opposed to details of money, manpower, stores and equipment – that is quite significant.

The next few weeks saw Robert pursuing his campaign in the south-west and, at the end of July, his cause was unquestionably furthered by an event in England – the death of Edward I at Barrow-in-Furness, probably from dysentery.

In death, Edward became much more popular than he had been in life. He had been feared by those around him as a violent and capricious man. His incessant demands for money to pursue his wars had brought his country close to civil war in 1297; a conflict that was only avoided when English society became united behind the king after the defeat at Stirling Bridge. He spent years endeavouring to acquire Scotland by force of arms, only to have to offer very easy terms to achieve peace, of sorts, in 1304 and then have the settlement unravel after only two years. All he had really achieved was an atmosphere of bitterness and mistrust between two countries which had – by the standards of the later Middle Ages – got along together rather well.

Edward I was buried with suitable pomp at Westminster Abbey, but the inscription on his tomb – *Malleus Scotorum* – was added 300 years after his death. Nobody would have called him 'Hammer of the Scots' in his own lifetime. Edward had – so it is said – demanded that his body be boiled and the carcass stripped so that his bones could be carried at the head of his army, either as it progressed through Scotland in search of Robert the Bruce, or on Crusade to the Holy Land. Whether he made such a demand or not, nothing came of it. The army he had raised was disbanded before the end of August.

EDWARD II

The new king, Edward II, took his father's body back to London. He has been the subject of a great deal of criticism for not carrying the war to Bruce with suitable vigour, but he really had more pressing matters to attend to than a relatively minor insurrection in a remote part of Scotland. The army that his father had raised was costing a fortune, and it was not clear what it could achieve. It could never hope to catch Robert's modest army operating as a single force. Splitting it into smaller parties to scour the countryside might seem like a good option, but that was likely to further irritate a local population that was not very taken with Plantagenet rule in the first place. Worse still, there would be the possibility that a detached part of the army might encounter Bruce and be defeated.

On a more positive note (for Edward anyway), Bruce had so many domestic enemies that there was every chance that he might be destroyed by the Comyn and MacDougall families with little or no aid from English resources at all. However, that was not a chance that Edward was going to take, and several senior officers were left to pursue the war against Bruce. In the meantime, he had to manage the business of taking over the core components of his domains, England and his lordships in France.

The former was relatively straightforward, although time-consuming. There would have to be a parliament, and he would have to take the homage of hundreds – or even thousands – of individuals and institutions, and do something about the state of the royal finances since his father had left enormous debts and expensive commitments.

These debts could not be met without the income from Edward's French possessions and he would have to make the necessary arrangements to give suitable homage to the French King for his estates, just as Alexander III had done to Edward I for his properties in England. This was a tortuous process of prolonged negotiation to ensure that the rights of the King of France were fully protected and that the dignity of Edward's kingship was not undermined.

The new king had no intention of abandoning the destruction of Bruce and the conquest of Scotland, but presumably he was not convinced that Aymer de Valence was making good enough progress.

De Valence was still in post on 17 September, but by the end of the month he had left Scotland and been replaced by John of Brittany, who was confirmed as Edward's lieutenant for Scotland on 13 September.

BRUCE CONTINUES HIS CAMPAIGN …

It would be easy to see the improvement in Bruce's standing after that point as a direct result of the change in the English administration, but although John of Brittany was not the most active or effective leader, the day-to-day business of the war was a matter for local leaders and garrisons. Unless Edward could find the money and personnel to increase the striking-arm element of the garrisons there was little that could be done to hamper Bruce. Large bodies of men-at-arms were needed to pursue him, and even greater numbers to enforce Edward's administration beyond the immediate vicinity of towns and castles. Edward and his officers understood this, but there simply was not the money to pay for it and, even if there had been, there was little prospect of recruiting enough men-at-arms for the task.

The garrisons themselves were secure, although this was more a matter of Robert's policy than their own strength. He simply did not make any effort to capture castles or towns for the first year and more of his campaign. He was certainly managing to draw men to his colours, because after a series of operations in Galloway that drove his opponents to seek shelter across the border in Cumberland, Robert was strong enough that he could divide his forces.

James Douglas continued the fight across central Scotland while Robert moved north to take on the Comyn family. In a sense, this was an internal Scottish conflict caused by the murder of John Comyn of Badenoch at Dumfries, but it is an oversimplification to think of it as just a civil war. The Comyns and their allies were leading figures in the English administration – they were regional officers with extensive powers. Even if John Comyn had not been killed, Bruce would still have had to deal with them if he could not persuade them to join his cause. The Comyns had served John

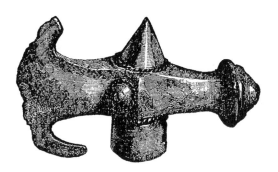

Balliol conscientiously throughout the first phases of the war and Alexander III and his predecessors before that. They would be taking an enormous risk if they were to reject the allegiance that they had given to Edward I in 1304, and were hardly likely to jump ship unless Robert had something incredibly valuable to offer them, which he did not.

Towards the end of the year, Robert was manoeuvring around the north-east. It was an unusually cold winter, rations for the troops were hard to come by and Robert himself was taken ill with an ailment that would bother him periodically for the rest of his days and which Barbour later attributed to spending too much time in the wilds. A number of small actions made little impression on the general situation, but on Christmas Eve, Bruce revived enough to lead his men to a sharp victory over the forces of John Comyn, Earl of Buchan (not to be confused with John Comyn of Badenoch – they were cousins).

This battle – probably no more than a few hundred men on either side – was a major advance for the Bruce cause. Buchan left his earldom and went into exile in England, while Robert's army devastated the countryside, lifting supplies, destroying stores and livestock, but most importantly driving out any who were loyal to the Comyn family. It was an object lesson in what could be expected for any region that resisted Robert's will. It was a barbaric act, but not unusual in the practice of war. Edward I had done something similar back in 1296 with the destruction of Berwick. Reports of the episode – Barbour calls it the 'herschip [hardship] of Buchan' – will have lost nothing in the retelling.

The 'herschip' had two effects: it naturally discouraged resistance to Robert's rule, but it also undermined confidence in the English administration. What the people wanted from government was, first and foremost, a stable administration that gave them the security to get on with their lives – something medieval people called 'good lordship'. A foreign occupation would inevitably be unpalatable to some degree, but if the quality of government was good and the administration of justice fair and reliable, it would be accepted over time. That would occur more easily if the mainstay of government – the earls and barons – were local men with their fingers on the pulse of the community.

Buchan was certainly ravaged, but agricultural areas recover quickly from scorched-earth tactics. Robert now had a very considerable range of estates of differing sizes that he could use to reward his own followers. In granting them estates, he gave them the opportunity to bring in their own dependants and associates to repopulate the area and make it a secure territory for the Bruce cause.

The possession of Buchan gave Robert a degree of political credibility. Increasingly, he was able to build a civil government, administer courts and collect rents and taxes. It improved his military situation as well. He now had a relatively secure hinterland from which he could expand to the west and north with no real fear of invasion. His domestic enemies in the north-east had been dealt with, an English invasion over land would be an enormous undertaking and likely to run out of supplies before it got too far north, and an invasion by sea would be foolhardy as well as ruinously expensive. Robert could now safely turn his attention to Ross, Caithness and Sutherland.

... AND GAINS AN UNLIKELY ALLY

The responsibility for resisting Bruce in the far north of Scotland now rested on William, Earl of Ross. William had been responsible for turning Robert's wife, daughter, sister and brother over to Edward I and all four of them had suffered dreadfully, so there was no love lost between them. On the other hand, Robert was a pragmatist. If he had to fight every inch of the way to gain control in the north, it would prevent him pursuing his cause elsewhere.

Equally, William's position was not strong, and Robert was obviously a major threat in the east. Clearly, Robert was the superior commander and was able to enlist a greater force, so if William wanted to retain his lands – not to mention the relationship between his head and his body – he would either have to obtain massive support from Edward or reach an accommodation with Robert. The latter might seem an obvious course of action, as Robert's strength was localised, but sooner or later he would have to face up to the power of Edward II and that might well be the end of him.

Caught between the proverbial rock and hard place, the Earl of Ross took the only action that might sustain his own position. He wrote to Edward to say that he had had no choice but to make a truce with Robert until Whitsun (2 June). He claimed that he had gathered his own forces and those of Sutherland and Caithness and kept them in the field at his own expense for two weeks, but Robert's force was so much greater that he would have been defeated to no good purpose.

It is not impossible that the three earldoms of Caithness, Ross and Sutherland could have provided 3,000 men, but it is unlikely that they would all be armed or trained adequately to deal with a superior army. It is, however, extremely improbable that Robert could have found anything like

3,000 men of his own, or that he would have been able to feed them if he had. The earl's entreaty to Edward rings a little hollow, but clearly Robert's army was a serious threat and at least appeared to be capable of remaining in the field for some time.

The Earl of Ross does not seem to have considered depending on the security of his castles long enough for Robert to be forced to abandon a siege for want of rations. Of course, he may have felt that he did not have the wholehearted support of his people. There are clear signs that Robert was popular with the wider community but, perhaps more pressingly, the people of Ross, Caithness and Sutherland would have been all too aware of what had just happened in Buchan.

The Earl of Ross did not finally abandon the Plantagenet cause until October, when he made homage to King Robert, was formally forgiven for any crimes against the king and his family, and became, from that point on, a stalwart of the Bruce cause.

ABERDEEN SECURED

The summer of 1308 was a very profitable one: the town of Aberdeen was seized and the castle taken after a siege of about four weeks. However, there is no evidence to suggest a close fight with catapults and ballistae. It is quite possible that the castle fell to a simple storming or some kind of deception, but it is, perhaps, more probable that the castle was surrendered on terms, since there would be small chance of Edward II's administration being able to mount a successful relief.

Surrender agreements were a common device for resolving sieges. The garrison would be allowed to leave with life, limb and liberty intact; they would not have to pay the ransoms that were customary when taken prisoner and their honour would be unsullied. In the meantime, by setting a date for the castle to surrender if there was no relief column, both the besiegers and the defenders could benefit by the arrangement. The defenders could bring in supplies and avoid starvation, and, by the same token, the besiegers could turn their attention to other projects rather than having to keep their force standing by.

Securing Aberdeen was a great boon for Robert. He now had, for want of a better term, a capital. It would be much easier to import arms from the continent, communicate with other kings, which was desirable – and with the Pope, which was vital.

The killing of John Comyn of Badenoch in a church had inevitably brought about Robert's excommunication. He could – and did – plead that there were extenuating circumstances and that he had acted in self-defence, but until his excommunication was lifted he would struggle to achieve religious recognition for his kingship. Worse yet, he was at war and might be killed in battle, in which case, as an excommunicate, he would go to 'hellfire and eternal damnation' – a rather more threatening prospect in medieval life.

ROBERT'S LIEUTENANTS

While Robert made the north his own, his lieutenants made great progress in the south-west. In both parts of the country, the same policy was observed in relation to castles. Once they had fallen they were not garrisoned – they were 'slighted'. As a rule, this did not mean destruction, just casting down a portion of the wall, or perhaps the gatehouse, to make the castle indefensible.

Installing garrisons would have meant a steady reduction in the field force and it also required a system for providing the men with supplies and wages to discourage desertion. The field force, on the other hand, could be held together with the prospect of loot or the ransoms of prisoners. A garrison would also have to resist the temptation to extort or steal from the community if Robert's administration was going to develop a better reputation than that of the Plantagenets. Moreover, placing garrisons would give Edward II's forces stationary targets to be eradicated and this would not be good for the military or political credibility of the Bruce cause.

The Efforts of Edward Bruce and James Douglas

The campaigns led by King Robert's brother, Edward, in Galloway, and by James Douglas, in west central Scotland, were built on hard and bloody actions on a relatively small scale, but it is misleading to think of them as 'guerrilla' leaders. Their battles were mostly conventional – just not very big.

For Edward Bruce, there was a clear political agenda. If his brother was able to make good his claim to the throne, Edward would inevitably become a very important figure in the Scottish political landscape. More than that, Robert had no son and his wife was a prisoner in England, as was his daughter and heir, Marjorie. It might easily happen that Robert would die – he had already been very ill at least once – and Edward Bruce might end up as king.

His campaign in Galloway was only successful in the sense that it pushed the English onto the defensive. The castle garrisons were no longer able to impose Edward II's government, but they had not yet fallen to Edward Bruce's army. The majority were still in English hands at the end of 1309 and the last would not fall until 1313.

James Douglas's position was rather different. He became one of the Bruce's greatest supporters – but that easily might not have been the case. His father had been forfeited for supporting the Balliol cause. James had petitioned Edward I to be restored to his father's barony in Lanarkshire and had been turned down, so his only hope of recovering his family heritage was to join Bruce.

According to one of Edward's officers, Douglas made an approach 'bleating for peace', which he had rejected. If he had accepted Douglas into

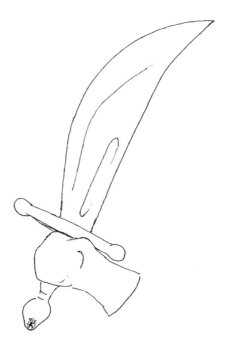

Edward's peace, he would have deprived Robert of one of his key officers. Instead, Douglas became an implacable opponent.

Edward I had granted the Douglas barony to one of the more senior men in the occupation government, Sir Robert Clifford, who had installed a small garrison in the castle. One of Douglas's first actions was to drive them out. According to Barbour, the action took place in early 1307 when the Bruce party was in a sorry state, but modern historians are more inclined to date the action to 1308. However, Barbour is very clear that it happened at a time when the Bruce side had no great strength, so perhaps it really was a 'one-off' event in 1307. Either way, Douglas chose to act on Palm Sunday, when he could be confident that the people of the village and the bulk of the garrison would be in the parish church, St Bride's.

As the 'proper' heir to the barony, Douglas was able to call on the services of some of his father's tenants, in particular, one Thom Dicson. Dicson sent word to the other 'gud' (prominent) men of the community and persuaded them to give their allegiance to Douglas as their native lord. Douglas's plan was to catch the garrison, only thirty in number, at their devotions, but the operation started to miscarry when one of Douglas's men called out a battle cry prematurely. Dicson drew his sword and set about the enemy, keeping them occupied until the arrival of Douglas and his men.

There was a short, sharp fight and all of the garrison were either killed or taken prisoner. Douglas immediately marched on the castle, a distance of about 1 mile, and he was able to enter unopposed. The garrison had left only the cook and the door porter who, unsurprisingly, offered no resistance. The prisoners from the fight at the church were brought to the castle and beheaded.

Collecting all the arms and armour that could be found, Douglas's men piled up all the provisions that they could find in a great soggy mass of flour, wine and malt, before setting the castle alight and withdrawing from the area. The 'Douglas Larder', as this engagement is known, was an exercise in terror, a message to all the men who served in the garrisons of the occupation government.

Destructive raids were a regular part of medieval warfare, as much in Scotland as anywhere else, but Douglas could not, in any case, provide a garrison himself, nor could he have supported one in the midst of one of the most effectively occupied parts of the country.

THE BATTLE OF BRANDER PASS

In August 1308, Robert Bruce carried his campaign into the west, seeking out the Lord of Argyll, John of Lorn. Aware that Robert would have to take a narrow path between Loch Etive and Ben Cruachan (which Barbour believed to be the highest mountain in Britain), John set an ambush. The resulting action is known as the Battle of Brander Pass.

By now, Robert was too experienced a commander to fall easily into a trap and he divided his force in two. He gathered his archers into one body and sent them up the side of the mountain, under the command of James Douglas, to take up a position uphill from the enemy. Robert led the rest of his men toward the ambush area, receiving just a few casualties from rocks rolled down the hillside by Lorn's men. As Robert's force closed with the enemy, the archers under Douglas made their move and trapped Lorn's men, inflicting heavy casualties, while Lorn watched the battle unfold from a galley in the loch.

Barbour thought that Lorn deployed at least 2,000 men in the battle, which seems rather large. However, at some juncture in 1307 or early 1308, Lorn had informed Edward II that he had 'only' 800 men under his command, 500 of whom were being paid for out of his own pocket, and he was receiving no help from the Barons of Argyll. Lorn would have had nothing to gain by inflating the number of troops available to him, in fact, quite the reverse. If he had been able to mobilise the support of the local barons in the face of a threat from the Bruce party, he might well have been able to put 2,000 men in the field. There seems to be no contemporary estimate of the size of Robert's army, but it would seem unlikely that he would be able to bring off an operation of this kind without having a substantial army under his command.

Brander Pass effectively completed Robert's destruction of the major Scottish families who were allied to the English administration, but a good deal of the country was still under occupation and land-holders who lived in those areas could not avoid discharging their military obligations without the risk of being forfeited of their estates.

A number of Scots served for wages in English garrisons – in fact, the small garrison at Peel in Livingstone seems to have consisted entirely of Scots, although that is exceptional. The rest might amount to a couple of hundred in castles spread across the country. Some served in order to simply make a living; some were men who had been driven out of their estates by the Bruces and whose best hope of recovering their lands was to support the English.

This was far from being a lost cause, even as late as the summer of 1314. Although the Bruce party was increasingly dominant across the countryside and the number of towns and castles in English hands was diminishing steadily, Robert's position was still very precarious. If he and his brother were to be killed in battle – or captured, which would certainly lead to their execution – the Bruce cause would be finished and men who had decided to stick with the English could reasonably expect to recover their property.

A PARLIAMENT AT ST ANDREWS

Even so, the Bruces were in the ascendancy. In 1309, Robert was able to hold a parliament at St Andrews. This was an important event in several ways. A good deal of the deliberations were focused on justifying Robert's accession to kingship, largely by denying that John Balliol's installation had been valid in the first place. It also generated two diplomatic letters to the Pope: one from the Scottish clergy and the other from the nobility stating their unqualified support for the kingship of Robert Bruce.

On a purely military level, it demonstrated that Bruce was starting to provide a conventional civil government and he was able to gather his supporters with impunity, just a short distance from the significant English garrison at Cupar. Just as importantly, it was evidence that his diplomatic efforts were beginning to bear fruit.

The other significant item on the agenda was a letter from Philip, King of France. Philip's letter discussed the long-standing friendly relations between Scotland and France and how well he regarded Robert himself – so much so that he suggested they should join together in a Crusade to the Holy Land. This was not quite an outright recognition of Robert's kingship, but it was probably as close as Philip could go, given that Robert was still an excommunicate. Robert replied that he had quite enough on his hands right at that moment, but once he had defeated the English and secured his kingdom he would be only too happy to join in.

Perhaps the most critical point about the St Andrews Parliament is that it made it more realistic to see the struggle as one between the kingdoms of Scotland and England rather than one man's struggle to achieve ascendancy. Bruce was still a long way from having the whole country behind him, but he was certainly the only viable route for Scottish independence.

ROBERT HEADS FOR ENGLAND

Bruce did not have it all his own way; in January 1312, he tried to mount a surprise attack on the town and castle of Berwick. The attackers had constructed ingenious scaling ladders, which are described in some detail in the *The Chronicle of Lanercost*, the chronicler asserting that he had seen these with his own eyes. The ladders were made of boards secured by knots in two lengths of rope, but the head of the ladder consisted of a large iron hook with a hole in the end which could be balanced on the head of a spear. The hook could then be lifted up to the wall and hung on the parapet.

However, the attack was a failure: the defenders were alerted by a dog barking at the Scots. Robert was not in a position to commence a formal siege, and so Berwick remained in English hands for another six years.

Elsewhere, operations proceeded more successfully. Although the counties of Lothian, Roxburghshire and Berwickshire had very strong garrisons, Robert was still able to mount expeditions through those areas and increasing numbers accepted the risk of forfeiture, presumably confident that the Bruce cause would win in the end.

Robert was then able to take the war into England. He kept very strong discipline among his

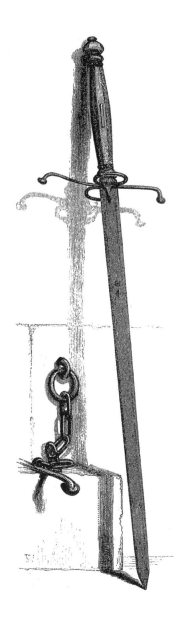

troops and prevented them from plundering the countryside as long as the communities paid large – although not crippling – ransoms to obtain truces for a few months at a time. Robert probably thought that these actions would bring Edward II to the negotiating table, but he was very much mistaken. Edward was infuriated, but not in the least moved by the plight of his subjects in Northumberland and Cumbria, and no more so when the raids became more ambitious and penetrated into Yorkshire.

But if these operations had no real political impact on Edward, they did have other benefits for Robert. Carrying the war into the enemy's territory was good for his prestige and credibility among his people – if there had to be a war at all, so much the better if it was being conducted in someone else's fields. They also gave Robert a structure for his military establishment.

Calling men out to perform army service was one of the ways in which medieval kings demonstrated their political status and power. Robert could – and did – turn out troops to serve at sieges, but these were largely passive affairs which depended mainly on starving the garrison until they were prepared to make terms. Marching into enemy country was more exciting, and the only way Robert could have prevented looting and disorder (which he did well) was to pay his troops. He certainly raised very large sums as ransoms for towns and communities and the money went somewhere – his treasury was always empty, so it is a fair bet that it was spent on wages.

ENGLISH LOSSES

Although many castles were surrendered by arrangement, this was not always the case. Early in 1313 King Robert laid siege to the town of Perth, one of the few towns in Scotland with any kind of fortification, although, of course, many – like Edinburgh or Aberdeen – had a castle physically adjacent. After about a week, the Scottish King led his army away from the town as though he had decided to abandon the siege, but returned under cover of darkness. Robert led an assault party which swam the moat, climbed the walls on ladders and entered the town on the night of 7/8 January.

Perth was the sole remaining English garrison north of the Forth and its loss was a severe blow to the credibility of the occupation. A French knight in Robert's company was immensely impressed at his determination to wrest every bit of Scotland from the enemy, astonished that the king should risk his own life to recover 'ane wretched hamlet', which says something about French perceptions of one of Scotland's most important towns. As a matter of policy, Robert slighted the fortifications, but would seem not to have demolished them completely, since Edward Balliol was able to set his men to extemporising makeshift but effective repairs in August 1332, after the Battle of Dupplin Muir.

Just a few weeks later, the English occupation suffered another serious loss when the town and castle of Dumfries were surrendered to the forces of King Robert by Sir Dungal MacDouall, who had been a staunch opponent of the Bruce cause, on 13 February. At some point that summer, the great military camp that Edward I had built at Linlithgow also fell to the Scots.

The writing was on the wall for the remaining areas under occupation, and in the early part of 1314 the powerful castles of Edinburgh and Roxburgh both fell to the Scots. The former was taken by stealth. The castle garrison had been contained for some time, but it was an extremely strong place and progress was at a dead stop. The commander of the besieging force, Sir Thomas Randolph, Earl of Moray, was approached by a man of the town who claimed he knew a secret path up the cliff to the west of the castle. He was as good as his word; he and Moray led a party up the path and over the wall. They set upon the garrison and provided a diversion while men from the town stormed the gate.

THE STIRLING CASTLE SIEGE AND LEAD-UP TO BANNOCKBURN

This left just two castles in English hands in central Scotland. One – Bothwell – was not terribly significant, but the other – Stirling – was regarded as a crucial asset. Perched on the top of a steep crag, it was almost impossible to take by storm and, overlooking the first point at which there was a bridge over the River Forth, it was of major strategic value. Stirling came under siege at much the same time as Edinburgh and Dunbar, but some historians have assumed that it was under siege by the spring of 1313. This is not the case; it still does not appear on a list of castles that Edward II's government considered to be at risk as late as October/November 1313.

Either by genuine mistake, or as a means of adding drama to his narrative, Barbour tells us that Edward Bruce laid siege to the castle at Lent in 1313, but it was almost certainly the following year. A compact was agreed whereby the garrison would surrender if it had not been not relieved by Midsummer's Day 1314. Local treaties of this nature were not unusual; Dundee had probably fallen to the Scots on similar terms in 1312. The value of such an arrangement to the garrison was largely one of comfort and security. As long as the compact was in place, they would be able to collect or receive supplies as required rather than undergo the privations of a close siege for months on end, and they would be guaranteed safety when the agreement expired.

For the besiegers, the compact would allow the force conducting the siege to be redeployed elsewhere. In 1313, Stirling was not seen as being particularly at risk from the Bruce party, but by then the Plantagenet administration in Scotland generally was becoming increasingly insecure.

EDWARD II FIGHTS BACK

In the hopes of restoring the situation, Edward started planning for a major expedition to Scotland as early as the winter of 1313. The size of his army – and that of Robert I – has been the subject of much debate.

Barbour's figure of 30,000 Scots and 100,000 English cannot be taken at face value; they were intended as literary, not literal, figures in much the same way that we might say 'millions' when we really just mean 'a large number'. Compared to most English expeditions of the fourteenth century, there is remarkably little written record pertaining to the army of 1314, but it is likely that Edward had between 15,000 and 25,000 men under arms, of whom perhaps 2,000, or at most 3,000, would have been men-at-arms.

The Scottish Army is generally believed to have been of the order of 7,000 infantry and 500 cavalry. The latter figure is not a very good indication of the number of men-at-arms in King Robert's army, since many of the nobles, including the king himself, fought on foot. Most historians have described the 500 Scottish horsemen as being 'light' cavalry. This is misleading; the only account that mentions the Scottish cavalry at all is Barbour, whose epic work *The Bruce* is by far the most detailed contemporary biography of any medieval European king.

Barbour tells us that the Scottish cavalry were on 'licht' horses, but we should not take this too literally. Having said in the preceding line that the cavalry were well-armoured 'in steel', Barbour may simply mean that the horses were 'mettlesome', or at a pinch that they were commonplace cavalry chargers rather than the destriers favoured by the very richest nobles, but perhaps 'licht' just fitted the tenor and meter of the poem.

Most of the infantry on either side carried polearms of some description, chiefly spears. The English Army had a larger proportion of archers, but the longbow had yet to be recognised as the devastating, battle-winning primary weapon it would prove to be at Dupplin Muir, Halidon Hill, Poitiers and Crécy. Like the spearmen and the men-at-arms, the archers of each army would have been indistinguishable to one another. The oft-repeated assertion that Scottish archers used a shorter bow than their English counterparts is firmly based in Victorian romance.

The compact between Edward Bruce and Sir Philip Moubray was almost incidental to Edward II's plans – he had been intending to mount a great expedition into Scotland for some time – but the arrangement may have been central to the plans of King Robert. According to Barbour, Robert was dismayed when he heard of Edward Bruce's compact, but that may not have been the case. Barbour is always at pains to tell the reader that Edward Bruce – though courageous and loyal – was a very rash individual. However, that does not really accord with his career as a rather successful military commander. Barbour's assertion is really more a matter of enhancing Robert's wisdom and restraint in comparison to his brother. It has been taken for granted that Robert did not want a major confrontation with Edward II's army, let alone a large battle, but that is by no means certain. Robert was a cautious commander, but he was prepared to offer, accept or even force battle if the situation merited it.

Edward II's army left Berwick on 18 June and marched on to Falkirk, by way of Edinburgh. These were long marches, and the English Army must have been somewhat fatigued in comparison to the

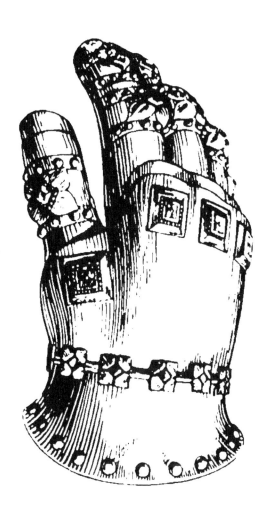

Scots. King Robert had been gathering and training his army at Stirling for some weeks, so his men would be fresh for the fight – should there be one.

This is an important point: Edward II and his commanders had been on several expeditions in Scotland, but actually bringing the Scots to battle had proved to be a difficult task. Experience would suggest that there was little chance that the Scots would stand and fight unless they could be trapped, and no real chance at all that they might actually force a battle.

THE BATTLE OF BANNOCKBURN, 23–24 JUNE 1314

Although roundly condemned for his actions on 23 and 24 June at Bannockburn, Edward actually behaved in a sensible and circumspect manner. As he drew toward Stirling, he detached two formations of his heavy cavalry. One of these was sent to effect a technical relief of Stirling Castle – the terms of the compact agreed in the initial siege required a relief column of at least 300 men-at-arms – the other, to ascertain the location of the Scottish Army. Both of Edward II's formations were strong enough to be committed to battle should they encounter a suitable opportunity.

One formation attempted to take the road through the New Park, an enclosed hunting reserve, where they met with a force of Scottish spearmen blocking an area known as the Entry, the point at which the road entered the woodland of the park. The topography, possibly supplemented with small pits to deny access to the flanks of the Scottish formation, funnelled the English advance so that they could only engage head-on. Unable to force their way in among the spears and harried by Scottish archers, the English force turned around and made its way back to the main body of the army.

Immediately before this action, King Robert performed one of the exploits for which he was to become famous. An English lord, Humphrey de Bohun, spotted Robert unattended and seemingly without his lance, the primary weapon of the fourteenth-century cavalryman. Seeing an opportunity to put his name into the history books and win the battle before it had really started, de Bohun launched himself at his target. King Robert, who was 40 years old, in the prime of life, and probably a much more experienced fighter than de Bohun, evaded his assailant at the last moment and smashed an axe through his head. Unfortunately, de Bohun had succeeded in one of his objectives – he had got himself into the history books …

The other English detachment fared no better. They were observed by the Scots as they made their way across the carse (the fertile floodplain of the River Forth) toward Stirling to relieve the castle, and King Robert sent the Earl of Moray to obstruct them. Seeing Moray's force moving down on to the plain in the vicinity of St Ninian's Church, the English commander decided to fight, even drawing his own force back to allow the Scots to come onto better ground for the horses. This proved to be a poor choice of action. The cavalry charged, but could make no headway against Moray's men, who had formed up in a tight schiltrom, or close circle, with spears facing out in all directions. Eventually the cavalry had had enough and withdrew, leaving the dead and prisoners behind them; some heading toward Stirling Castle and the rest to rejoin the main body of the army which was now marching on to the low ground (or carse) to the east of the Scottish Army, about 2 miles south of Stirling Castle.

Edward's choice of the carse as a camping and concentration area for his army has attracted a great deal of criticism, but there were several perfectly sensible considerations that led him to this decision. Establishing his army in an area bounded by streams gave an element of security – a high priority, given that a night attack by the Scots was thought possible. It would be very difficult for the

Scots to approach the English camp without being seen, and difficult for them to cross either stream in the face of even a modest sprinkling of guards. Just as significantly, the streams would provide adequate water points.

Obviously, men require water, but the needs of the thousands of horses and oxen would be more pressing – one can explain to a man that he will have to do without water for a day, but one cannot explain that to a horse. Wherever the English Army camped for the night, there would need to be water in abundance, but they could not afford to make camp at any great distance from the Scots if they were to have any chance of delivering an effective attack the following day.

Medieval armies on the march moved very slowly indeed. If Edward's men were camped even just 3 or 4 miles from the Scots – not enough in itself to prevent a night attack – they would likely need two hours, at the very least, to deploy and march on the Scottish positions in the morning.

The events of 23 June favoured the Scots. There were two actions, each of them successful, in which casualties had been light, and the English commanders had lost the reconnaissance battle because their army was down on the carse and therefore completely under observation, while the Scots were camped on higher ground out of sight of the enemy.

It would seem that Robert was not absolutely committed to offering battle the next day. He had evaded the English before without seriously damaging his prestige or credibility, and the defeats already suffered by the English would be excellent propaganda material. Better yet, the prestige of Edward II was bound to be tarnished – he had led a large army to Scotland and suffered two reverses on the same day. If Robert chose just to retire and avoid battle, Edward would fail to achieve anything at all for his effort.

According to Barbour, Robert was still undecided about his next step when Sir Alexander Seton entered the Scottish camp. Seton had been one of the lords who had declared for Robert in 1306, but subsequently defected to the English. He now

defected back to the Scots, telling Robert that there was great confusion, depression and disarray in the English camp and that this was the moment to throw caution to the winds and attack.

Edward II and his officers do not seem to have contemplated the possibility of a conventional daylight attack by the Scots at all, although this was not so cavalier an attitude as it might seem. The English had been at war with the Scots almost continually for the better part of twenty years. To date, their chief tactical difficulty had been in forcing battle on the enemy. There had been very few general engagements during that period, but the English commanders had good reason to be confident that their troops would be more than a match for the Scots on a conventional battlefield. In reality, the terrain in which the English now found themselves would probably have encouraged confidence in their situation.

Historians have made much of the soft, marshy nature of the ground and have pointed out how much of a hindrance this would have been to the English cavalry. However, a carse is not a bog, and while in the wintertime it is generally wet underfoot, in the middle of summer it is firm underfoot, although traversed by streams. Interestingly, none of the contemporary commentators identified the marshy ground as a tactical factor in the fighting, although clearly the Bannock Burn, 'an evil, deep, boggy stream', as Sir Thomas Gray called it, was a serious obstacle for the English troops once the battle had turned into a rout. Contemporary writers seem less surprised that infantry had defeated cavalry than that they had done so on dry, hard, flat ground.

The nature of the terrain is an important issue if we are to understand the course of the main part of the battle. The cavalry on both sides needed firm ground to fight on, but so did the infantry. In particular, the large formations of Scottish spearmen would have needed solid ground to advance any distance in good order. To achieve success, spear formations needed to keep their 'dressing' – the intervals between ranks and files – very rigidly. Like the classical Greek phalanx, the schiltrom was vulnerable when disordered. The 'hedgehog' effect of the spears simply would not be successful if the spearmen could not present a consistent mass of spearpoints to the enemy.

Edward's choices have attracted criticism, but so too have those of Robert Bruce. Superficially, it would seem that he was extremely rash to carry the fight to the enemy. However, there were several good reasons for him to do so. Naturally, King Robert had a far better understanding of the capabilities of his own army (and indeed Edward's army) than we can possibly hope for. Evidently, he was convinced that the troops were up to the job. Equally, the Scottish troops were convinced that Robert was up to the job – he and his lieutenants had led them very successfully for several years.

Although combat was a risky undertaking, avoiding combat might also be dangerous. The fights at the Entry and near St Ninian's on the late afternoon of 23 June would still play well with the Scottish public if Robert chose to withdraw before Edward's army, but it would not constitute a major political event. Few people would be drawn to the Bruce cause if the 1314 campaign consisted of two successful, but relatively minor, actions followed by a retreat into the north while Edward's army laid waste the south.

Robert had gathered a very large army by Scottish standards, especially bearing in mind that a fair slice of southern Scotland was still not under his control. If that army did nothing more than retire before the English, it might prove difficult on subsequent occasions to persuade men to leave their farms and businesses to camp out in the fields for days, or even weeks, avoiding the enemy. Further, if Robert did not defeat a major English field army he would have a long struggle to gain recognition of his kingship. Both Edward I and Edward II had made it perfectly clear that they had no interest in reaching a negotiated settlement that did not involve English sovereignty over Scotland. The only way to drag Edward to the negotiating table would be through victory on the battlefield, and Robert might never have such a good opportunity again.

His army was well trained, well armed and confident, and his enemy was on the plain before him. Obviously, the sheer scale of the English Army must have been a cause for concern, but Robert had already taken steps to ensure that it was not a cause for alarm. When a reconnaissance party had reported the approach of the English in great strength, he had passed word that the English were indeed in great number but also in a state of disarray, encouraging his own troops to believe that an attack, if delivered, would be successful.

Whatever the rationale behind King Robert's decision, there is no doubt that the Scots did move to attack the English. This is really the crucial factor in understanding the main part of the engagement. Sir Charles Oman – and many others since – chose to see the battle as an opposed river crossing, with the English cavalry attempting to force a crossing of the Bannock Burn against a row of four circular Scottish schiltroms whose flanks were protected by numerous 'pots' to trap unwary men-at-arms. There are a number of problems with this interpretation, not least the fact that all of the contemporary material clearly indicates that the Scots took the initiative and none suggests that the English cavalry came to grief trying to cross a muddy stream so that they could throw themselves, in suicidal fashion, onto Scottish pikes. Given the extensive English experience of fighting the Scots, this would have been a most unlikely approach to battle. The vulnerability

of schiltroms to archery had been amply proven at Falkirk in 1298, and there is no reason to assume that English commanders would not have kept in mind the lessons of their victory.

King Robert's plan was to attack the English and drive them back onto their own baggage trains and into the lower reaches of the Bannock Burn where it flows into the River Forth. To achieve this, he would need to have mobility and secure flanks. The circular schiltroms of Falkirk would have been very difficult indeed to manoeuvre and, just as importantly, would have only presented a very small front compared to a linear formation, meaning that fewer men would have been able to bring their weapons to bear on the enemy. Assuming a similar number of ranks in each unit, the difference in effective frontage would be at least three to one in favour of the rectangular, linear formation. To make his plan effective, King Robert's army would have to contain the English, prevent them from evading his advance or turning his flanks, and, crucially, prevent them from deploying their archers.

Edward's selection of camping ground made all of these things possible. The two burns that bounded his camp had provided his army with security in the night, but they now prevented effective redeployment. Neither the Pelstream Burn nor the Bannock really represented that much of an obstacle to a single, reasonably fit person, but the banks are both soft and deep, making a difficult barrier for a body of men or horses.

Although Edward and his officers were probably surprised that the Scots took the initiative, they were not put into a state of shock. The Scots marched down to the plain from their assembly area (roughly where Bannockburn High School stands today) in three columns, halted and then each column turned to the left or right to present lines facing east. Two of the columns – one under Edward Bruce and the other under the Earl of Moray – were somewhat in advance of a third, larger column under Robert. At this point, the Scottish Army famously knelt to hear Mass and confess, so that any who might fall in battle would die in a state of grace.

On the other side of the battlefield, Edward is reported to have observed the Scots kneeling and asked if they were going to beg for mercy. Making confession on the eve of battle or hearing Mass immediately beforehand were normal procedures in the Middle Ages, but there may have been a military significance to doing so at Bannockburn. The Scottish Army had to descend a fairly steep escarpment to deploy on the carse and the dressing of the units would undoubtedly have suffered as they did so, having the units kneel to hear Mass would allow the unit commanders and the junior leaders

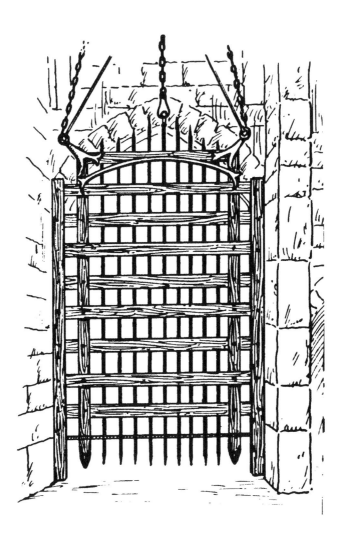

to make good any deficiencies, pushing men into the right position and ensuring that the ranks and files were well ordered before the unit rose to make its advance.

The poet Barbour is alone among the contemporary or near-contemporary commentators in describing the Scottish Army as having four main battle formations. All of the other writers are agreed that there were only three. This discrepancy is probably political in origin. While other writers list the Scottish formation commanders as the king's brother, Sir Edward Bruce Earl of Carrick, Sir Thomas Randolph Earl of Moray, and Robert himself, Barbour allocates a fourth formation to Sir James Douglas. For Barbour – writing sixty years or so after the event – it would be inconceivable that someone as prominent as Douglas would not have had a major command, but in 1314 Douglas, although already a famous man-at-arms, was not yet a person of great political significance among the Scottish nobility. His rise to political prominence would come about after the death of Edward Bruce, at the Battle of Faughart in 1318. Also, when describing a fourth column, Barbour was perhaps inventing a role for Walter the Steward, who he tells us was joint commander of that column with Douglas. One would have to wonder why only one column would need a second commander. However, there is possibly a simple explanation: Walter the Steward would eventually marry Robert's daughter Marjorie, and his son would become King Robert II in 1371 – Robert II was Barbour's patron …

According to the Lanercost chronicler and Sir Thomas Grey – a professional soldier whose father was taken prisoner in the fight between the infantry of the Earl of Moray and the cavalry of Sir Robert Clifford near St Ninian's Chapel – two Scottish formations advanced in line abreast, occupying almost all of the frontage between the Pelstream and Bannock Burn, with the third formation between and behind. By the time the Scots had approached to within a couple of hundred yards of the main body of the English Army, a skirmish line of sorts had been put together, but was easily swept aside by the advance of the spearmen.

A hastily mounted cavalry attack by the Earl of Gloucester failed to turn the tide and, as the Scots advanced, the English were compressed into a smaller and smaller area, thus denying them space to manoeuvre freely. At this juncture – according to Barbour, and he is the sole source for this part of the action – a body of English archers was deployed to the left flank of the Scots and began to inflict heavy casualties. However, before they could make any serious impact on the situation, the Scottish cavalry, under Sir Edward Keith, crashed into their ranks as they were still assembling and drove them from the field. With the archers gone, the Scots were able to press on with vigour until the English Army started to disintegrate. By the close of battle hundreds, perhaps thousands, were drowned in the Bannock Burn, and many more lay dead on the battlefield or had been taken prisoner.

Edward was dragged from the battlefield by his bodyguards, who took him to the castle, where the commander was prepared to admit him and let the siege continue, but made the point that the castle must fall sooner or later if it was not relieved, and where was such a force to come from? There were still probably more English than Scots in the vicinity, but cohesion of the English Army had disappeared. Edward's army had effected a technical relief of the castle, in the sense that the force had come within the specified distance and also in the sense that the castle garrison had been reinforced – if only with fugitive men-at-arms from the fighting of the previous day – but, in reality, the garrison commander had no choice other than to surrender his charge to King Robert at the earliest opportunity.

Although he had achieved a stunning victory, Robert was not free to give all his strength to the pursuit. For one thing, his army was exhausted, but also the large numbers of English soldiers who had survived the fighting might yet be regrouped under an effective leader. It would be very unlikely that they would seek to renew the battle, but they would be able to cause great damage if allowed to reorganise.

Since taking shelter in Stirling Castle was not a viable option for long, Edward now had to move away as quickly as possible. Accompanied by his household knights and men-at-arms, he made his way around the rear of what had been the Scottish position that morning and headed for Dunbar Castle, home of Patrick, Earl of Dunbar, who, like his father before him, had been a supporter of the Plantagenet cause.

The journey to Dunbar was not a matter of a short pleasure ride through the countryside. As Edward left Stirling, his departure had not gone unnoticed and a party of Scottish men-at-arms under Sir James Douglas pursued him, although Douglas's force was far too small to challenge Edward's entire household. At Dunbar, Edward was supplied with a boat which took him to Berwick, whence he continued his journey home by ship.

It has been suggested that the Earl of Dunbar would have done very well to seize Edward and give him up as a prisoner to Robert. However, Dunbar probably did not have the necessary strength to take on Edward's remaining retinue. Further, by letting Edward leave he probably gained a good deal of credibility with the Plantagenet family, which eventually stood him in good stead when he was obliged to defect, briefly, to the cause of Edward III in 1333, despite the fact that he had, by then, been an active and effective adherent to the Bruce cause for nearly twenty years.

Bannockburn was the worst defeat of English arms in the medieval period. The siege and capture of the baggage trains of King Edward and his magnates must have provided an immense amount of plunder, augmented, if not surpassed, by the many ransoms taken. For King Robert, it was an endorsement of his rule: with the exception of Berwick, the few castles still retained by the English were surrendered and he at last had the whole country in his hands. However, he had not yet won his war. He would have to mount several campaigns in England and Ireland before eventually forcing the Treaty of Edinburgh–Northampton on the government of Edward III in 1328.

More myths have attached themselves to this battle than any other Scottish engagement, and some of the events of the action may have been invented by Barbour for the sake of a good tale. There is no contemporary evidence whatsoever for the great band of 'small folk', beloved of Scottish commentators, who – according to Barbour, but no other contemporary writer – threw themselves into the battle just as the English Army was collapsing.

More recent embroideries are much less excusable. Charles Oman's tortuous bending of the material to justify his assertion that the English attacked the Scots has been influential for more than a century. Despite being thoroughly debunked by Reverend MacKenzie as long ago as 1913, it was still being repeated as recently as 2014.

Modern romantic interpretations tend to give a picture of unarmoured Scottish peasants wresting victory from a vast body of English knights in a swamp, even though contemporary material is quite clear that the Scottish Army consisted of experienced and well-equipped troops, who advanced on the English Army and engaged them on solid ground. The worst offence against reason is the widely held belief that the Scots were saved at the last moment by the intervention of a great company of Knights Templar careering over a hill and crashing through the English ranks. This tale has been rehashed by the writers of novels masquerading as non-fiction work, and often enough that this completely imaginary intervention is now on the verge of becoming an accepted part of the battle.

GAINS AND LOSSES FOR ROBERT AFTER BANNOCKBURN

Among the fruits of victory, Robert gained more than just the money from ransoms, considerable as his share undoubtedly was. Several major figures in English society had fallen into his hands and he was able to secure the release of his surviving family members from English prisons, including his spouse, with whom he might hope to create an heir.

What he did not achieve, however, was recognition or peace. The war would drag on and on, and for the next two years, most of the action would be in the north of England, although there were occasional incursions by English forces.

In 1315, Robert laid siege to Carlisle, but found it was too hard a nut to crack and he had to abandon it. The following year, the man who had commanded the successful defence there, Sir Andrew Harcla, led a company of men-at-arms – 300 strong according to Barbour – on a foray into Eskdale and was intercepted by a Scottish force of rather lesser strength, under Sir John Soulis. The English force would very probably have contained a number of Scottish knights and men-at-arms who had lost their estates through their opposition to Robert. Harcla's force was defeated and Harcla himself taken prisoner. He was released for a ransom of more than 1,000 merks (a merk, or mark, was one-third of £1, or 13s 4d), an enormous sum in the fourteenth century.

A Bruce King of Ireland?

Another major development in the nature of King Robert's war occurred in 1315. His brother Edward and Thomas Randolph, Earl of Moray, took a large, powerful force to Larne in Ireland and set about a campaign to unite the various petty kings and great lords behind a single issue – the defeat of English power. For Robert, the issue was probably more a matter of opening a second front, diverting the war away from Scotland and preventing Edward II from obtaining men and food from Ireland to support campaigns in Scotland. It had the added benefit of keeping an army that would largely be self-supporting.

After a year of campaigning, Edward Bruce had himself crowned King of Ireland, and for a while it looked like he might make a success of the project, but he could never gain a wide enough base of support among the greater Irish lords and eventually was killed at the Battle of Faughart in 1318.

SUMMER, 1317

While Robert and the Earl of Moray were supporting Edward in Ireland, back in Scotland, the war still spluttered away. In 1317, Sir Robert Neville of Raby, a prominent leader in the north of England, led a strong force of men-at-arms, including several Scots who had lost their lands through supporting the English occupation and a number of Gascons from Edward II's lordship in France, on a raid into Berwickshire. A Scottish force under Sir James Douglas gave chase and defeated them in the vicinity

of Berwick. Barbour tells us that Sir James considered this to have been the hardest fight he had ever been in. Neville, known as the 'Peacock of the North', was killed, along with a large number of his men, including Raimond de Caillou, a noted paladin and nephew of the notorious Piers Gaveston, who was thought by some contemporary chroniclers to be Edward II's lover (this is still debated among historians).

The Earl of Arundel was commissioned by Edward II to conduct operations against the Scots in the early summer of 1317. In May, a flotilla of five ships manned by over 300 'armed sailors' landed to the west of Inverkeithing, in Fife, to lay waste to the countryside to try to undermine the credibility of Robert. Initially, the force enjoyed some success. The Sheriff of Fife, who had, in common with sheriffs throughout England and Scotland, responsibility for the immediate response to local military threats, led a force against the enemy but was quickly repulsed. By chance, the Bishop of Dunkeld, William Sinclair, was in the vicinity, visiting one of a number of parishes along the Firth of Forth that were detached parts of his diocese. The bishop, armed and armoured and at the head of a company of sixty men-at-arms, met the sheriff, upbraided him for failing to defeat the English and led his own and the sheriff's men into the fight.

The bishop's intervention turned the day for the Scots, and the English were driven back to their ships with considerable losses.

That same summer, a large force of English men-at-arms was assembled by the Earl of Arundel in person as part of a series of operations that may have been timed to take advantage of the absence of King Robert and the Earl of Moray, who were still campaigning in Ireland in their effort to make Edward Bruce the King of Ireland. Barbour puts the size of this force at nearly 10,000 men, many of whom Arundel equipped with axes, intending to completely level Ettrick Forest. (This is obviously a massive exaggeration, and the figure has a literary, not literal significance: it merely denotes 'a very large number'. Barbour's intention was probably that the reader should understand that this was a major initiative, not simply a raiding party.)

In the absence of Robert, Sir James Douglas had responsibility for the safety of the country, and when the English crossed the border, Douglas was at his newly built manor at Lintalee on the Jed Water. Douglas had a party of fifty men-at-arms and a large company of archers. He was aware that the English Army would have to take a road through a particular wooded location, and where the road entered the wood there was a broad clear space on either side, which narrowed to a spot where the woods were less than a stone's throw from the road. Douglas hid his archers on one side of the road and his men-at-arms on the other. When one of the English commanders, Sir Thomas Richmond, came into view, Douglas launched his attack, killing Richmond himself. Caught between the onslaught of Douglas on one side and the arrows of the archers on the other, the English force quickly quit the field.

This was not the end of Arundel's operation, however. Barbour tells us that a portion of the force was detached to find a camping ground for the main body of the English Army. This party, commanded by a clerk (in the sense of a cleric or priest) named Elias, had selected a site and settled down to eat when Sir James Douglas – possibly returning from the fight at Lintalee – fell on them, inflicting heavy casualties.

At least one account differs radically from Barbour. According to an unpublished manuscript translated by Joseph Stevenson and cited by Professor Duncan, Douglas had made a fortified camp at Lintalee and had given it a garrison of 200 men-at-arms. On the approach of Arundel's army, the Scots fled and the camp was seized by a party of men under Elias. As Elias' company sat down to enjoy the meal that they had found laid out on the tables, the Scots returned and put them to the sword before attacking the main English force under the command of Arundel. Professor Duncan has drawn attention to the remains of earthworks on a promontory overlooking Linthaugh, on the Jed Water. If the unpublished account is accurate in its description of Douglas's establishment and the nature of its garrison, we might be best to think of it in similar terms to the peels erected by the occupation government at Linlithgow and Selkirk. These were not castles in the normal sense, although the civil functions of the sheriff were certainly exercised from Linlithgow Peel around 1300–14, the purpose of a peel was primarily military; it was to provide a permanent depot and quartering for the retinues of men-at-arms that were required to support the occupation government. Douglas's establishment presumably provided a secure base for his *comitiva* (retinue) for the defence of the border.

BERWICK UNDER SIEGE ONCE MORE

One part of Robert's kingdom continued to be occupied for some years after Bannockburn, the town of Berwick, which at that time was one of the most significant ports in the British Isles. Edward I had destroyed it in 1296, but it was so well situated to take advantage of the wool trade that it had recovered very quickly, although it never really regained its full position.

After at least one previous attempt, Robert laid siege to Berwick at the end of March 1318. He was approached by one of the burgesses of the town, Peter (or Piers) Spalding, with an offer to allow the Scots to enter by climbing the area of the town wall for which he had responsibility. This was a normal arrangement in walled towns throughout Europe. The Crown might supply a garrison for the castle and perhaps men for the defence of the town, but the burgesses and other residents were expected to take an active part in the event of a siege.

King Robert suspected a trap, but took the chance. On the appointed night, Sir James Douglas led his men into the town, winning it after some very heavy fighting. The castle was effectively a separate institution militarily and was not taken that night. However, without the facilities of the town's harbour, the garrison could no longer be sustained from England by sea and the general military ascendancy of the Scots was such that there was no prospect of pushing a relief column through by land. The town had fallen, but the castle garrison held out until June.

Recovering Berwick was a great boost for Robert's prestige, but its loss was a serious blow for Edward II. His inability to protect such an

important acquisition reflected badly on his prestige and credibility. However, bad as the situation was, it deteriorated rapidly thereafter, with the capture of three significant castles in England: Harbottle, Wark and Mitford.

The Battle of Myton

Defeat on this scale had a temporary unifying effect on the political community in England. Edward II had been on very bad terms with several of his magnates, but he was now able to prevail upon several of them to raise a substantial army, and in the summer of 1319, he laid siege to Berwick town and castle. The garrison withstood several assaults, but all sieges must be successful eventually, unless the besieging force leaves the scene.

Moray and Douglas had a force in the area, but were not prepared to offer battle. Instead, they moved south into Yorkshire, hoping to draw Edward away from Berwick to protect his subjects (it was rumoured that the Scots were aiming to threaten the safety of Queen Isabella, who was residing at York). This gambit had little effect until the Scottish Army was confronted by an English force at Myton.

The battle that ensued is generally dismissed as a farce. There were so many clergymen in the English Army that it was referred to as the 'Chapter of

Myton'. However, this is a little misleading. Virtually all priests – or monks, for that matter – were men of the gentry or nobility, and training to arms was part of their education. The force was not incompetent or unarmed, it was just no match for the army of Douglas and Moray, and was easily defeated.

When news of the battle reached Edward II at Berwick, the newfound political unity that had enabled him to form an army at all evaporated. His supporters left in a hurry and Edward had to abandon his siege – another blow to his prestige and another feather in the cap of Robert and his lieutenants, including his son-in-law, Walter the Steward, who had commanded the defence of Berwick town and castle with some skill.

Robert's armies could now roam through northern England pretty much at will. With no army and no hope of raising one, Edward had no choice but to accept further humiliation and seek a truce from Robert. After some negotiation, he was able to get a truce for two years from Christmas 1319.

PEACE AND PLOTTING

There may have been peace, of sorts, between the kingdoms, but Robert did not yet have complete security. Although he had acquired great prestige through his military successes, the simple fact was that he was still a usurper. He had arranged declarations and Acts of Parliament that supported his kingship, but he was not really the true and lawful heir of Alexander III – that was Edward Balliol, son of the deposed King John.

The Declaration of Arbroath

In 1320, Robert produced the most significant declaration of his kingship and of Scottish independence – the Declaration of Arbroath. It is a key document in Scottish history and is famed for the assertion that Scots would never submit to the English. It is a fine propaganda statement, but it is more than that; it was a means of ensuring that any of Robert's subjects who still harboured sympathy for the Balliol cause would have to nail their colours to the mast of the Bruce party – and to be sure that they did so, Robert demanded that they hand over their seals to be used on the declaration.

At a parliament after Bannockburn, Robert had issued a decree inviting any Scots who had not yet come to his peace, on the understanding that they would reject and abjure any commitment to any other king – which, of course, really just meant the King of England! The invitation was not open-ended; the men and women in question had a year to make their minds up but, after that, anyone who had not entered Robert's peace would be forfeited with no hope of reconciliation. Many of his former opponents had already made the move, of course, and a few more did so at this point – a few were even accepted after the deadline had passed.

The De Soulis Plot

Not everyone who took advantage of the offer of peace or handed over their seals for the Declaration of Arbroath was genuinely committed to the Bruce cause. Robert still had no son, and all his brothers were now dead. If he were to die without a son – which, by this time, must have looked more likely than not – the Balliol cause might be resurrected. If he was to be killed in a coup – and the plotters planned that he and his lieutenants would be – it was quite possible that Edward Balliol could be installed as king without too much difficulty.

The plan was discovered, however, and the plotters were tried and executed. The prosecution tried them on the basis that they were trying to replace Robert with Sir William de Soulis, although in fact any claim that de Soulis might have had to the throne would have been tenuous, to say the least.

Barbour tells us that there were 360 men-at-arms ready to strike as soon as the king was dead and that these men were each 'in their own livery' – an early use of the term, which indicates that they were all men who were (or had been) of some substance and with their own heraldic devices. These were undoubtedly men who had lost their heritages due to their support for Robert's enemies, whether English or Scottish, and expected to be restored to their lands if Edward Balliol could be put on the throne.

It is possible that the conspiracy took place without Edward II's knowledge, but it seems rather unlikely. A few years after Robert's death, Edward Balliol would make a serious attempt to make himself king with the aid of troops raised by men who had lost their Scottish lands and titles. They were known as 'the Disinherited' (in fact, some of them had become disinherited because of their involvement in the de Soulis conspiracy).

Edward III (after Edward II had been deposed and murdered in 1327) later claimed that his father was not party to the Balliol campaign. However, he clearly took a great interest and it is quite possible that, in both cases, Edward Balliol had undertaken to accept the sovereignty of English kings if they would help him to the throne. That may seem rather weak-willed, but it was actually the basis on which his father had been king and on which

King Robert's grandfather would have ruled if the Great Cause of 1290–91 had gone in his favour.

The Earl of Lancaster

The truce that had been agreed after Myton in 1319 was observed reasonably well, but as soon as it was over, Robert's forces were back in action, crossing the border at will and demanding ransoms or blackmail from the counties of northern England as far south as Richmond and Darlington. Edward II had entrusted the defence of the north to Thomas, Earl of Lancaster, who chose to do nothing at all to obstruct the three Scottish columns under Moray, Douglas and Walter the Steward. Lancaster had been communicating with Robert – or at least his officers – in secret for some months. It is not absolutely clear what Lancaster (and his co-conspirator, the Earl of Hereford) hoped to gain, although presumably it would involve the effective removal of Edward II from power and the erection of a regency of some sort with Lancaster pulling the strings. What he had to offer was recognition of Scottish independence and Robert's right to be king, although whether Robert set much store by Lancaster's plans is questionable at best.

Things did not go well for Lancaster or Hereford. When Edward II became aware of the situation he acted with an unusual degree of effectiveness and vigour. The two earls retreated northward to join up with the Scots, but were intercepted by a force under Andrew Harcla and were thoroughly defeated at Boroughbridge. Hereford was killed in the battle and Lancaster was captured and executed the next day.

Edward Strikes Back into Scotland

Edward II now made plans to invade Scotland once again, but before he could do so, Robert led another foray into England, this time as far as Preston and Lancaster, both of which he put to the torch as a challenge to Edward's authority.

Late in August 1322, Edward invaded Scotland with an army of over 1,000 men-at-arms, almost 20,000 infantry and about 1,500 hobelars. Hobelars were essentially mounted infantry, in the sense that they would dismount in order to fight in a general engagement. However, they did have an extensive mounted role, and as well as reconnaissance and foraging operations they could be used to 'pad out' a body of men-at-arms to maintain control of communities, or even possibly in an attack on infantry, although that would be a risky undertaking. This was an army of similar stature to the one that had been defeated at Bannockburn six years before, and substantially larger than the one that Edward had taken to Berwick in 1319.

Edward arrived at Edinburgh, having found the entire area stripped or burned in front of him. Robert I's adoption of a scorched-earth policy suggests a number of aspects about his view of Lothian and the south-east. That he was prepared to devastate it himself, if necessary, to deny it to the English, is fairly obvious, but there may have been a political dimension. He may have been making it clear to Lothian landholders that the price of any collaboration with a future English occupation government might carry a heavy penalty.

The dearth of forage in Lothian drove Edward II to retire after a week. Barbour tells us that the only foodstuff that could be procured from the county was one lame cow, abandoned by the retreating Scots some days before. Apparently, this sorry creature inspired the Earl of Surrey to call it the 'dearest beef I ever saw: it has cost us a thousand pounds or more'.

The withdrawal from Lothian was the cue for the Scots to advance from Culross in Fife, where King Robert had kept his army during the English incursion to harass and hasten their retreat. Part of Edward's army made a diversion to pillage Melrose Abbey, but was surprised by a force of men-at-arms under Sir James Douglas and driven off with heavy losses.

As Edward II made his way south, his army started to dwindle steadily; men saw the campaign as being at an end and chose to make their own way home rather than wait for the army to be formally disbanded. In the normal way of things, this would not have been a problem – in fact, it was generally an advantage, since if men had left the army they did not need to be either fed or paid, which would obviously save Edward a tidy sum. This time, however, it was very nearly a disaster. As Edward moved south, Robert pursued him all the way to Yorkshire and inflicted yet another sharp defeat on the English Army at Scawton Moor. Fortunately, Edward was not present; he had gone to Rievaulx Abbey and was lucky to avoid being captured, a fate that befell several of his senior nobles.

A TIME FOR TRUCE?

Robert returned to Scotland with spoils and prisoners, but really no nearer his objective of a perpetual peace treaty. He entered into secret negotiations with Sir Andrew Harcla, who had been a staunch supporter of Edward for years, but clearly despaired of his king ever providing stable leadership and peace for the north. Harcla was acting under his own initiative and presumably with the support of other

prominent men, but his actions were unquestionably treasonable. Edward became aware of his activity and promptly had him executed.

Removing Harcla did nothing to improve Edward's position; he now had to negotiate with Bruce himself. This was difficult because he could hardly recognise Bruce as king without accepting that neither he nor his father had any right to try to annexe Scotland in the first place. Equally, Bruce could hardly accept any agreement that did not recognise his position. After tortuous negotiations, a truce was agreed for thirteen years – probably the best that could be hoped for under the circumstances, but far from ideal for Robert. He was not an old man, but he was certainly not young and his health was not good. He might not live long enough for a son to grow to maturity.

In a sense, nothing had changed. There was peace, but there was also the prospect that the war might be renewed at any moment. There would have to be a major change in the political situation in one or other country before there could be any major progress.

The Death of Edward II and Opportunity for Robert

The change came with the deposition and then murder of Edward II in 1327. Edward's queen, Isabella, and her ally and lover, Roger Mortimer, raised a small army and invaded England in 1326 with the avowed intention of deposing Edward and replacing him with his young son, also Edward. Within weeks Edward II's government had collapsed and he was little more than a fugitive, before being captured in November and forced to abdicate in favour of his son in January. After this, he was known as Edward of Caernarvon.

This was an opportunity for Robert. He declared that the truce was now at an end, due to the fact that one of the principals was no longer the king of his country, and cross-border actions started up almost immediately. This led to perhaps the greatest campaign of Robert's reign, although there were no battles and he stayed some distance away from the action, such as it was.

Isabella and Mortimer dispatched the newly crowned Edward III northwards with a large army. Whether they really thought he could achieve anything where his father and grandfather had failed, or whether they just felt they ought to be taking some action and it was helpful to have the king out of their way, is open to question.

The campaign of 1327 was a disaster. The Scottish Army under Moray and Douglas outmanoeuvred their opponents again and again. The English Army became dreadfully demoralised and, one night, Douglas came within a whisper of capturing Edward.

Enough was enough for Edward, and he retired to York as his army disintegrated around him. However, the worst was yet to come, and in August and September Robert's armies roamed across the north of England, taking ransoms from those who could find the money and the goods and chattels of those who could not. Isabella and Mortimer had no money to raise another army, and even if they could raise the cash, there was no guarantee that they would be able to recruit the men. There was no other option than to start negotiations for a proper peace treaty – not a truce this time, but a formal end to the war.

The negotiations took some time and there were many genuinely complicated issues, not least the fate of those who had lost estates in either country through their loyalty to their king. In an attempt to ensure that his heir's position would not be threatened in the future, Robert procured the hand of Edward III's sister, Joan, aged 7, for his son, David, who was just 4 years old. Even by the standards of medieval diplomacy this was young, but it was not unheard of at the time.

England and Scotland had been at war for almost all of the previous thirty years and a degree of ingrained animosity had developed, but it was not inevitable that things should stay that way. The two kingdoms had had remarkably good relations in the past, and there was nothing revolutionary about Scottish princes marrying English princesses and vice versa; that had, after all, been the plan for Margaret of Norway, granddaughter of Alexander III, and Edward of Caernarvon, the previous English king.

A TREATY MADE

The treaty that Robert had fought for was finally made on 17 March 1328 but, little more than a year later, on 7 June 1329, he died at his country house at Cardross. He had been a great king in many ways

– most famously in war, of course, but he had also given his attention to the wider business of kingship. He built no great castles and set up no new towns because none were needed, but he was attentive to matters of trade and justice as a king should be.

Perhaps the finest testament to his ability and achievement came from – of all people – an English herald at Edward III's Court known as 'King Robert'. When asked who he thought was the finest knight in Christendom, he replied, 'King Robert of Scotland', for his courage, determination, skill and achievements despite adversity. At that time, heralds were expected to be serious warriors, so when 'King' Robert said he would 'defend his choice with his body', he really meant it, and nobody felt like accepting his challenge …

3

KING
ROBERT'S
SCOTLAND

A good deal of northern and western Scotland is little changed in appearance since the time of King Robert. The roads are more numerous and much better, but the mountains and the coastline are much the same now as they always were. Some terms used in medieval documents have changed their popular meaning – today, a forest is an area of woodland, but 700 years ago the connotation was 'wilderness' or 'the great outdoors', regardless of whether it was covered in trees. The armies that fought King Robert's wars passed over mountains and through forest when they had to, but most campaigning took place in the most densely populated and agriculturally productive parts of the country.

The prosperity of the whole community rested on farming and the export of produce – mostly wool, leather, hides, honey and linen – so it is worth examining Scottish society, if only to see what the Scottish people were fighting for in their wars with the English. The wars may have been fomented by powerful landowners, but they could not be conducted without the support of the community as a whole.

HIERARCHY AND ADMINISTRATION

The social administration of Scotland in the days of King Robert I would seem not to have differed very greatly from conditions in England before the reforms of Edward I. The king's laws and policies were implemented by a network of sheriffs and lords, assisted by their bailies and sergeants, who between them maintained law and order, administered justice, collected taxes, rents and customs, and carried the responsibility of leading the men within their jurisdiction in times of national emergency – usually war.

These local potentates were supported by a wider group of minor nobles and, increasingly, successful commoners and burgesses exploiting the land market. Essentially, the nobility and gentry were rentiers (landowners, or 'middling folk'), retaining little if any land directly under their own management and relying instead on the rental income of their properties. They provided the membership of criminal and civil juries, in addition to their immediate landholding rights, which might themselves involve a degree of criminal jurisdiction.

Effectively, the king provided for the needs of the men (and, to a lesser degree, women) who carried out his government by means of salaried office, in some cases, and by grants of land, temporary or heritable, in others. Naturally, the proportion of society that comprised the social and economic elite was only a tiny fraction of the population as a whole. For the vast majority of King Robert's subjects, the reality of life was farm work – in all likelihood, nine out of ten people spent some part of their life in farming and, without question, the entire economy depended upon it.

Popular histories of Scotland (and some scholarly ones as well) offer a grim picture of universally impoverished peasant farmers living in the thrall of (probably rapacious) lordly nobles and gentry in a primitive agricultural and largely pastoral economy. In that picture, the instability of medieval Scotland – wars with England; domestic wars; plagues among the people; epidemics among sheep, cattle and even chickens – conspiring with poor climate and soil conditions, worked to prevent any real improvement in the wealth of the society. This is not a view supported to any great degree by the archaeological evidence, nor really by the documentary record of the period. Much of our perception of agricultural Scotland before the 'improvers' of the eighteenth century is coloured by the fact that so much of the earlier landscape is described to us by the improvers themselves – in their estate plans, diaries, letters and, most importantly, in their publications.

Improving landlords had an agenda to pursue. Part of the justification for improvement inevitably lay in criticising the practices of the past. The commercial success that usually accompanied improvement demonstrated its validity in terms of increased production, but the prejudices of the improvers have helped to further obscure the realities of life for the majority of Scottish people in the medieval period. In the eighteenth and nineteenth centuries, the mania for agricultural improvement swept away almost all of the traces of earlier farm practice in the race to replace the 'old ways' with modern, scientific methods.

The work of historians, unsurprisingly, tends to focus more on the actions and fortunes of the great and good. This is an unfortunate, if inevitable, consequence of trying to unravel the story of medieval Scotland as a political entity, as the narrative of a succession of kings and the kingdom they ruled. Any study is bound to be preoccupied primarily with the leaders of men, and consequently there is a tendency to overlook the men that they led. The lives of the vast majority of medieval Scots are completely lost to us in terms of detailed biographical data of individuals. Scotland has no equivalent of the Paston Letters (a collection of correspondence between a medieval Norfolk family and their acquaintances, which illustrates their rise from peasantry to landed gentry over just three generations) to shed light on the lives of the lower gentry and their servants.

There is no shortage of evidence of the existence of the lower gentry and the peasant classes. The gentry figure in the witness lists of their lords' charters; the peasants are listed as part of the stock referred to in those charters. Concerning the gentry, we can ascertain a good deal from documentary evidence, primarily charters granting feudal land tenure. The granting or confirmation of a charter tells us about the land that the recipient of the charter enjoyed and the rights that went with it. The charter also makes clear the services that the recipient was expected to perform in order to fulfil his contractual obligations. The rental due to the superior depended on custom and the relationship between lord and vassal, rather than any concept of the real commercial value of the contract.

LANDOWNERS AND TENANTS

In a feudal society all land was, in theory, owned by the king. The landholder's property was, strictly speaking, merely rented, but on a perpetual and heritable lease and at a fixed rate. Unsurprisingly, the holders of these leases were more enthusiastic about the perpetual and heritable aspects of the contract than they were about the inherently impermanent nature of a lease. As far as they were concerned, they owned their land with free and secure title so long as they performed the stipulated services appropriate to that property.

The great landowners leased their estates from the king, in order to lease them out to their own vassals and dependants who, in turn, let them to farming tenants. At some point in this chain of contracts, the nature of the payment (*reddendo*) changed from money and military service to one of labour and produce. Once land was granted by inheritance, the next tenant would naturally seek the erosion of any obligations due to the feudal superior, and the easiest – though, in the long term, most damaging – way for the landlord to reward or influence his tenant would be to reduce those obligations.

Among the gentry and aristocracy, the 'rent' could be a purely symbolic payment – a pair of white gloves or a hawk, for instance. Some of these rents are rather more astute than first glance would indicate. The fairly commonplace inclusion of expensive produce, such as a pound of pepper or cumin, was effectively a hedge against inflation. Fixing payment at the weight, rather than the cash value of an expensive imported product must have paid dividends when the value of most European currencies as foreign exchange collapsed in the later fourteenth and fifteenth centuries.

Military service was similarly 'hedged' against inflation. The quality of equipment required to perform knight service rose steadily through the thirteenth and fourteenth centuries, but because army service was assessed in days of service rather than a cash equivalent, the increasing cost of military service in general, and knight service in particular, fell on those who served it rather than those who received it.

During the thirteenth century, the demand for military service dwindled due to the long period of peace with England and stability at home, but the militarisation of society that was engendered by the war with Edward I can be seen in the (relatively) large number of King Robert's charters that stipulate military service as an important part – sometimes the sum total – of service due to the king for the property.

The rents of tenant farms were generally of a much more realistic economic nature than the token payments levied for estate holdings, but the cost of appropriate military kit and the regularity of military service being demanded were obviously much less. The level of labour service attached to property diminished as commutation for cash payments became commonplace through the thirteenth century. The amount of unpaid labour that an individual had to perform on a lord's estate was an indicator of a person's status in the society.

The term 'class' would have been incomprehensible to medieval Scots, but they were keenly aware of 'status'. The rising incomes of the labouring classes allowed them to reduce their level of 'unfree' obligations, leading to a rapid decline in the number of people living in serfdom. Landowners were not in a hurry to give up rights of ownership over their workers, nor to lose labour services incidental to land they rented out, but the convenience of operating in a cash economy – even if rents were actually paid in produce – encouraged tenants to buy out their lord's rights if they felt they could make sufficiently profitable use of their time in pursuit of their own agenda. Obviously, they needed to make it cost effective enough to either supply a hired hand in their place to work the required days or negotiate the commutation of the labour into a cash settlement.

The extent to which a tenant enjoyed freedom from labour services on his landlord's property was an indication of the extent of his personal liberty, but it is important to bear in mind that our information really relates to the property in question, not to the person who worked that property. Labour service to be provided by a tenant was part of his rent and did not necessarily imply that the tenant was not personally free. The social position of the tenant was not an issue in this. When Sir Ingram de Guines became a tenant (with three others) of a property at Lamberton, he became liable for his share of the ploughing and harvest services due from that property to the manor of Ayton in just the same way that any non-noble tenant would become liable for the services attached to the property he or she leased.

The involvement of members of the baronial class in the agricultural land market as tenants of farms (or mills), as well as landlords, shows that farming was seen as a potentially lucrative venture. Interest in agriculture was not limited to the peasants and the baronage. Successful burgesses bought farmland to lease, not only for the profits of farming but to acquire an improved status in the community that would allow them to join the gentry.

However, not everyone fitted perfectly into our picture of the feudal pyramid. The general pattern of farm tenants and cottars paying rent to a lord was not absolutely universal. Proprietary farms existed, being the property of a number of 'heritors', whose children, as the name implies, would inherit their rights in the property. The inhabitants of such farms were not necessarily much better off than their tenant neighbours, but they obviously enjoyed security of tenure and freedom from labour services, heriots (material payments, for example, a horse or clothing, due to the lord on the person's death), merchets (a fine paid to their lord if they got married) and the other trappings of feudal inferiority.

SERFDOM AND PERSONAL LIBERTY

The economic advance of the lower orders of Scottish society throughout the thirteenth and fourteenth centuries is unmistakable, and the changes in servile status that allowed farmers to expand their enterprises are both cause and product of an improving economy. The charter terms of 'servi', 'neyf', 'bondi', 'rustici' and 'nativi' may have been nuanced terms with individual meanings to medieval Scots, but, if so, this information has not been recorded. The inclusion of some or all of these terms in land transactions may sometimes be little more than the preservation of legal formulae which had largely fallen into disuse. We might be better to regard these people as sitting tenants with a security of tenure that their children would inherit, rather than a completely servile class 'thirled' (tied for life) to the plough.

Neyfs or nativi might be thirled to the land, but they were not necessarily without rights or protection. For example, a landlord at Arbuthnott refrained from removing a serf – 'Gillandres the lame' – when he discovered that Gillandres was a long-standing acquaintance of the local bishop.

The social standing of servile status is impossible to clearly ascertain. Professor Duncan has identified examples of 'free' men marrying 'villein' heiresses in order to obtain a landholding. Perhaps the land was as much thirled to the villein as the villein was thirled to the land … The implication surely is that while the lord might own the land and the people who farmed that land, the land was not much use to the lord without labour. If the neyfs could not prosper in their relationship with their lord they might easily desert him for another. In the climate of a declining population, the new lord, keen to ensure that all of his lands were in production, would be unlikely to enquire too closely into the technical liberty of someone in search of a farm lease.

A lack of personal liberty did not need to be a sign of abject poverty. For example, in 1247, a burgess of Berwick purchased a neyf for 20 merks. This large sum is explained by the fact that the neyf in question was the grieve (manager) of Prenderguest Estate in Berwickshire and therefore a man accustomed to considerable responsibilities. As the grieve of the property, he would have far too much opportunity to improve his financial situation at the expense of his employer/owner if he was not adequately 'looked after'. The grieve may have been a 'slave' in the strictest sense, but he was not likely to have been poor.

The aristocracy may have been keen to protect their property rights over other human beings, but precisely what these rights meant in practical terms may not have been particularly clear to them, let alone us. The economic developments of the twelfth and thirteenth centuries and the extension of personal liberty in the fourteenth century may have made it genuinely difficult for both landlord and tenant to be sure of their rights and responsibilities. This may have been complicated by changes in lordship. A newly 'infeft' ('appointed', for want of a better word) lord would be unlikely to want to cause bad feeling among the tenants by demanding more of them than the previous incumbent – he would need the support of these men if His Lordship was going to be successful. Perhaps more importantly, the arrival of a new lord might be a good opportunity for the tenants to play down their responsibilities to the estate, claiming newly invented 'traditions' that their previous lord would not have recognised.

Quite why servile status should have started to disappear in Scotland as early as it did is open to question, but the influx of French, English, Flemish and German merchants and artisans who settled there in the twelfth and thirteenth centuries must have had some impact. The incomers were personally 'free', in the sense that they did not physically belong to another human nor were they obliged to give extensively of their time to tending a lord's fields. These people did not come to Scotland to be poor; they came because of the potential rewards of operating in a rapidly modernising and expanding economy. The success stories among the immigrants would surely encourage local Scots to aspire to the liberties and wealth of their new neighbours and to acquire a greater degree of personal liberty.

The lengthy war was a factor as well. Inevitably, there was a good deal of social disruption, but it would be difficult to justify demanding contributions – and, in the case of wealthier serfs, military service – to support a war of independence from people who were not going to be personally free once it was over.

Some quite modest landowners held their property directly from the king, and even some small tenants, although few were as humble as the group of 'king's husbandmen' who petitioned for an improvement in their tenure status in the early days of Edward I's occupation. These smallholders were seeking the same tenure rights as their counterparts in England, who had longer leases, which shows that Scottish husbandmen were aware of the different conditions in another country and were not shy of approaching the king to secure an improvement in their own status. Only a tiny proportion of smallholders were direct tenants of the king, of course, but most landowners would have this sort of tenant and it is reasonable to assume that baronial tenants would be likely to want any improvement in the conditions of royal smallholders to be extended to themselves.

THE LANDLESS LABOURERS

Below the smallest tenants there was a class of landless men who depended on labouring in other men's fields for their daily bread. This pool of labour was vital for the economy. Landless men had the most time available to undertake work for others, but terms like 'cottar' or 'husbandman' should not be seen as strict social stratifications; day labouring for someone else was potentially an important part of the income of many smallholders, as it still is in many parts of the country today.

Labour wages could also supplement the incomes of people who were not strictly members of the rural economy. Eyemouth in Berwickshire was founded as a trading port and fishing settlement to serve the priory of Coldingham, but of the fish bones recovered by excavation, the vast majority seem to have been caught in the summer months. This suggests that the villagers found harvest-time employment on nearby farms, since the inhabitants of the village were mostly landless cottars. Their lack of arable land is further indicated by a rental (rather later than the reign of King Robert admittedly, but there is no reason to assume any great degree of economic change in the intervening century), in which the nineteen cottar holdings are charged rentals comprising money and fish, but no agricultural produce.

Even within a small settlement like Eyemouth, there was some variety in the tenure of the inhabitants. Beside the cottars there were four freeholders, presumably farmers whose products could be processed in a local mill that had not been mentioned in an earlier rental. The main 'internal' enterprises of the township were fishing and brewing – four breweries existed; surely more than enough for the inhabitants of a village with only twenty-five houses.

THE ECONOMY

The rapid (by medieval standards) development of the economy in the thirteenth century changed the nature of Scottish society, but it was also part of what made Scotland an attractive proposition to its expansionist neighbour, Edward I of England. The lengthy Wars of Independence he engendered probably hastened the decline of servile status through the widespread disruption of the community that can often be caused by war.

If we reject the proposition that medieval Scotland was an uncommonly primitive and poverty-stricken society, we should be equally careful not to exaggerate the prosperity of that community. Almost without exception, visitors to Scotland paint a pretty bleak picture of both the land and the people. A French knight who appears in Barbour's *The Bruce* describes Perth – one of the most important, largest and wealthiest of Scottish burghs – as a 'wrechyt hamillet [wretched hamlet]', which at the very least tells us how Barbour (who had travelled to London and Paris) thought a foreigner might view a rather grand Scottish place.

The perceived prevalence of 'runrig' tends to give us an unrealistic picture of a standard format of farming practice in medieval Scotland. In the runrig system, the arable is divided into long parallel

plots or 'rigs' (hence 'runrig') and then allocated to individuals. An 'infield', under continual cultivation, then received all the manure, while outlying pastures were intermittently cultivated, with a head dyke separating the two.

The reality of agricultural practice was rather more diverse. The precise nature of each farm depended on its situation, local traditions and conditions. A parcel of good arable land might be set to less profitable pasture if the area in question was prone to military activity, because flocks and herds can obviously be moved more easily than standing crops or stored produce.

The purpose of runrig may well have been to collectivise labour, tools and plant (in the shape of draught animals) – a development that is unlikely to have been uniform, either in time or form, so we should not be surprised at regional or local variations in agricultural activity. References to runrig are common from the fifteenth century, but it had already been the most widely used approach for time out of mind.

The term 'infieldland' first appears in a fifteenth-century tack (lease) for Abirbrothy (modern-day Arbroath) in Angus, but infields were common throughout the east of Scotland. This field would receive the bulk of the manure and was sometimes referred to as the 'mukkitland'. Mukkitland would be more or less continuously cultivated, and in marginal areas the exhaustion of the infield beyond the capacity of dung to repair the damage would lead to the abandonment of the farm 'toun' (or steading) and the incorporation of its grazing into other farms.

If we accept that runrig was the common approach, we should remember the exceptions – demesne farming was not generally an important feature of land use in medieval Scotland, but it was not unknown. Unless the formation of rigs was going to cause a major improvement in the drainage of the field there would be no reason to adopt them, unless there was a reason to divide productivity on an individual basis. And why should a cottar with perhaps as little as 2 or 3 acres subdivide his field into narrow plots, given the labour involved in digging and maintaining deep furrows which would effectively reduce the size of his field?

BUILDINGS IN ROBERT'S SCOTLAND

When we consider the buildings in which people lived and worked, we again find a more sophisticated situation than we might expect. Unfortunately, the most common materials used for construction – turf and wattle and daub – do not generally survive well. Roman turf fortifications have been successfully excavated, but they were massive constructions built under professional supervision. The less substantial dwellings of medieval Scottish peasants have simply dissolved due to weather erosion and almost all trace of them has disappeared under more recent construction.

Chiefly due to the continuous occupation of farm locations, an unrepresentatively large proportion of the medieval archaeological work carried out in Scotland has been urban. The majority of the buildings investigated in both rural and urban settings have been wattle-and-daub constructions, but there is a considerable variety in the construction styles.

The nature of the materials did not mean that the houses were all hovels. The bishops of St Andrews owned a manor house at Stobo, near Peebles, to which they could retreat, and it is fair to assume that it was reasonably comfortable. Robert Bruce built himself a manor house at Cardross, so presumably a manor could be at least as comfortable, and even perhaps as prestigious, as a castle. Crown records refer to it as a manor, but a visiting diplomat called it a palace. Evidently, it could be a fit home for a king, even one as conscious of prestige as Robert I.

On a less exalted level, successful merchants like John Mercer or Eleanor Monkton would presumably like to enjoy the fruits of his or her labour. The appearance of someone's home – especially if it is his or her place of business – is an indicator of status. For example, an Inverness burgess who had expensive plank cladding added to his house, had it installed only on the wall facing the street where it could make an impression on the people of the town.

Meanwhile, an excavation at Inverness has revealed clay walls 'supported by vertical oak planks or staves', wattle and clay daub, and plank walls set into sill beams, all contemporary and in the same location. Similar work in Aberdeen showed an equal variety of construction methods, and also some houses built on stone sill work, which suggests a certain degree of permanency. This might well be a result of increasing prosperity and a considerable amount of redevelopment in the fourteenth century, but may just be a reflection of local fashion. Householders in the towns built according to taste and pocket – presumably rural freeholders (at least) did the same.

Excavation at Springwood Park in Roxburghshire has indicated sturdy cruck-built houses with stone walls to about 1m and a thatched roof to an apex of roughly 3m. Heather and turf were common roofing materials elsewhere, but heather is scarce in Roxburghshire and in an area of good agricultural land straw would be more likely.

RURAL LIVING

The more marginal the land, the greater reliance on beasts rather than crops, and the declining population of the fourteenth century would have made these marginal fields uneconomic in terms of return on labour. The fact that people were willing to invest such a lot of effort into poorer soil areas is indicative of the profitability of agriculture, but the reversion of these lands to pasture in the years after the plagues of the mid-fourteenth century should remind us that marginal farmland was not typical farmland.

Another factor in the reversion to pasture or abandonment of farms in the later fourteenth century may have been the succession of 'good years', when crops were relatively rich across much of Scotland. This would inevitably reduce the 'real' price of food, with consequences for farms that were only marginally profitable in normal market conditions.

Where occupation of a medieval farm has been continuous to the present day – and this must be the vast majority of them – development has obviously hidden any evidence of the past. The expanding use of very large prefabricated buildings around established farmsteads in recent times undoubtedly compounds the problem, and because of the rather insubstantial nature of wattle-and-daub construction many medieval sites probably go unrecognised as such. Enclosures and earthworks of the medieval landscape can also be mistakenly associated with the outlines of prehistoric ring houses that they happen to enclose.

While it is true that most people lived in small farm steadings of wattle-and-daub construction, there were people who did not. At least one stone-built village (Lour, in Peeblesshire) and one planned village (Midlem, in Roxburghshire) have been identified. The discovery of two substantial 'hall houses' at Rait and Morton would suggest a rising non-noble landowning class who could afford to invest in comfort as well as security. A nucleated village at Camphill, enclosed with ditch and rampart, indicates a degree of insecurity among the inhabitants, but it also suggests that they considered the effort of building these defences a worthwhile investment. That they had the resources to invest in such a project would further suggest that they were correct.

Not everyone lived on farms, of course. About 10 per cent of the population lived in towns, or burghs, which largely ran themselves. One of the functions of burgh administration was to set fair prices for necessities. The most important of these products were bread and ale. The pricing or 'assize' of bread and ale was effectively set by the price of wheat and of barley. Oats do not seem to have been the subject of assizes, save in times of dearth. The value of oats as a cash crop for landlords in east coast Scotland by early modern times has been amply demonstrated by T.C. Smout and A.S. Fenton, 'hardly a family north of the Tay not shipping grain or meal either coastwise or abroad'.

If the chief means of turning agricultural activity into cash lay in the cultivation of oats, there are questions to be asked about productivity. The traditional Scots proverb, 'Ane tae saw and ane tae gnaw, and ane tae pay the laird witha', is difficult to accept at face value. It claims that the return for the farmer amounted to three grains for each planted – one to sow for next year, one to eat and one to pay the rent. If a good return on oats was three grains for each one sown, how could farmers recover from abnormal contingencies?

If a return of three for one was the norm of cereal productivity, farm failure and abandonment would be much more commonplace. Possibly that level of return represents the minimum return necessary to survive and not the normal expectation of yield. It is, of course, important to bear in mind that what might seem to us an insignificant difference in yield between one year and another might be of considerable import to a medieval farmer; the difference between three for one and three and a half for one represents a margin of greater than 15 per cent, which is hardly trifling. If the production of a farm was sufficient to provide rent, seed and sustenance, and nothing more, there would be no money to make good the inevitable accumulated shortfall caused by accidental damage, unseasonable weather conditions or the passage of armies. Even the most minor crop failure would permanently undermine the economy and viability of the farm.

This did, of course. happen from time to time – whole settlements could go out of use – but that is comparatively rare, and desertion of a site is not necessarily a product of environmental factors. The village of Mow, in Berwickshire, for example, disappeared because the landowners sold off small pieces of arable land with extensive grazing rights to Kelso Abbey until there was not enough to service the flocks of the villagers. Changes in the weather, soil

exhaustion, market forces and depopulation due to war and plague also caused the abandonment of farms and villages, but this was chiefly from marginal lands.

The poverty that early visitors to Scotland describe was very real. The vast majority of people lived what would seem to us a life of unrelieved squalor. For the poorer members of the community, a poor harvest would mean a spell of serious deprivation at best and starvation at worst. The life of the medieval farmer in Scotland was not an easy one, but the same applies to farmers all over Europe. Scottish peasants may have been poor, but no more so than their equivalents elsewhere. Their personal freedom may have been a little more developed than the lower orders in other parts of Christendom, but it did not make them wealthier. On the other hand, the peasants' revolts of England, France and Germany have no counterparts in medieval Scotland, so perhaps the ordinary men and women of that society were better off than it would seem to us.

4

SOME MYTHS ABOUT KING ROBERT

It would take a very big book to deal with all of the myths that have grown around Robert the Bruce over the years, but here are a few old chestnuts – some venerable, some quite recent …

'King Robert was an Anglo-Norman …'

This is a description that needs some qualification, to say the least. In a general sort of a way, the term 'Anglo-Norman' is really redundant for anything to do with England after 1150 or so, and is therefore even less useful when applied to Scotland. The Bruce family arrived in Scotland in the mid-1100s and by the time Robert was born they had been part of the political community for 150 years – they were hardly a new fixture in the national firmament. Robert's early ancestors, going back six or more generations to Robert de Brus, 1st Lord of Annandale, are said to have come from France (although this is disputed by some), but by the time of Robert's birth there was a good mix of Gaelic in there too, on his mother's side.

'King Robert spoke French …'

This is almost certainly true, to a degree. We should certainly expect that Robert could read French in the same way that most well-educated British people of 100 or 200 years ago could read Latin. French was the language of literature, but it is difficult to imagine how anyone could grow up in thirteenth-century Carrick and Annandale without learning to speak both Scots and Gaelic; how else would they communicate with their neighbours, tenants and servants? Unless there was a great social upheaval in Scottish society between 1100 and 1300 that produced enormous changes in the linguistic constitution of the country, and yet made no mark whatsoever in the record, we must ask how it should be that if the Scottish nobility spoke French, the greatest – certainly the longest – piece of literature produced by their society was composed in Scots? Without question, Barbour's epic was written for the benefit of aristocratic audiences – and, self-evidently, they would probably have wanted to be entertained in Scots, not French.

'The Bruce claim to the throne was superior to that of John Balliol; the Bruces were cheated out of their inheritance by Edward I, who had received the homage and fealty of John Balliol ...'

Edward I had also received the homage and fealty of Robert the Noble (Robert's grandfather), and the balance of expert legal opinion at the time certainly favoured King John's arguments over the rather convoluted claims of the Bruce party.

'King Robert was elected king by a group of seven earls in an ancient Scottish tradition of regal inheritance ...'

That may sound very positive and patriotic, but it is not indicated by any evidence whatsoever; it is probably a complete invention. Robert was a usurper. By chance, the Balliol line came to an end with the death of King John's son, Edward, in 1354, at which point the Bruce family became the legitimate line, but not before.

'King Robert was saved at Bannockburn by the intervention of a band of Knights Templar, to whom he offered refuge from their persecution in France and England …'

There is no evidence whatsoever to support this increasingly popular 'tradition'. On the other hand, there is plenty of substantial circumstantial evidence against it. King Robert was an excommunicate and very keen to be readmitted to the solace of religion. The last thing on his agenda would be to offer any offence to the Pope. Further, the suppression of the Templars had occurred at the behest of the King of France, whose support was vital for Robert's diplomatic campaigns. Robert would have been ill-advised to encourage the Templars in any way, let alone give them shelter. Finally, the Templars of the late thirteenth and early fourteenth centuries are probably better thought of as an international property conglomerate rather than an operational military organisation. The senior officers were hardened by conferences and lengthy struggles in courtrooms rather than combat.

'Robert the Bruce was a turncoat …'

King Robert was the product of his station and time, the same as anyone else. The activities of his life were perfectly normal for a man of his rank. He endeavoured to protect and extend his family inheritances in both England and Scotland; he performed military and administrative services for his king; he hunted; he ran up debts; he gave to the Church; he hoped to go on Crusade and fight in the Holy Land against what Barbour calls 'God's foes'. The regularity with which Robert changed sides in the decade from 1296–1306 may seem remarkable to our eyes, but not particularly so in the eyes of his contemporaries. Very few Scottish nobles managed to keep their heads above water – or for that matter joined to their bodies – without a few judicious changes of allegiance.

'Robert the Bruce had leprosy …'

King Robert was certainly very ill on several occasions, but leprosy was feared beyond any other ailment and even kings would be forced into a solitary quarantine. Medieval people were very familiar with leprosy, even recognising that it could take two rather different forms. It would seem that the assertion that he suffered from this dreaded disease was no more than English propaganda.

DRAMATIS PERSONAE

Alexander Bruce, Dean of Glasgow	1285–1307, brother of King Robert I.
Alexander III	1241–86, King of Scotland 1249–86.
Alexander Seton, Sir	1266–1350, Governor of Berwick, took part in Edward Bruce's campaigns in Ireland in 1315, signatory on the Declaration of Arbroath.
Andrew Harcla, Sir, 1st Earl of Carlisle	1270–1323, military leader on the Scottish border.
Andrew Murray, Sir	1270–97, chosen as joint Guardian of Scotland in 1297 with Sir William Wallace, father of Sir Andrew Murray who married Christina Bruce.
Aymer de Valence	1275–1324, Edward I's military lieutenant in Scotland.
Christina Bruce	1278–1356, sister of King Robert I, first married to Sir Christopher Seton and secondly to Sir Andrew Murray (younger).

Christopher Seton, Sir	1278–1306, married to Christina Bruce, present at the murder of Sir John Comyn in Greyfriars Church.
Edward I	1239–1307, King of England 1272–1307.
Edward II	1284–1327, King of England 1307–27, known as Edward of Caernarvon after his abdication.
Edward III	1312–77, King of England 1327–77.
Edward Balliol	1283–1367, son of John Balliol.
Edward Bruce	1280–1318, brother of King Robert I, laid siege to Stirling Castle.
Elizabeth de Burgh	1284–1327, second wife of King Robert I, married in 1302, kept under house arrest from 1306 until 1314.
Henry Percy, Sir	1273–1314, 1st Baron Percy of Alnwick, fought for Edward I but rebelled against Edward II.
Isabella MacDuff, Countess of Buchan	Died 1314, held prisoner in Berwick from 1306.
Isabella of Mar	1277–96, first wife of King Robert I, died before he was crowned.
James Douglas, Lord of Douglas	1289–1330, chief commander during the Wars of Scottish Independence, known as Black Douglas to the English and Sir James the Good by the Scottish, signatory on the Declaration of Arbroath.

John (III) Comyn, 1269–1306, was murdered by Robert or
Lord of Robert's men at Greyfriars Church in
Badenoch Dumfries.

John Balliol 1249–1314, King of Scotland 1292–96.

John Barbour, 1320–95, author of many works including
Archdeacon of *The Bruce.*
Aberdeen

John Comyn, Earl 1250–1308, cousin of John (III) Comyn
of Buchan Lord of Badenoch.

John of Brittany, 1266–1334, was Edward I's military lieten-
4th Earl of ant before Aymer de Valence.
Richmond

John of Lorne, Lord Died 1316, set the ambush that resulted in
of Argyll the Battle of Brander Pass.

Malcolm Died 1307, executed by Dungal MacDouall
MacQuillan, when he arrived at Galloway with
Lord of Kintyre Alexander and Thomas Bruce, and
Sir Reginald Crawford.

Margaret of 1261–83, Queen of Norway, daughter of
Scotland Alexander III, mother of Margaret, Maid
of Norway.

Margaret, Maid of 1283–90, granddaughter of Alexander III,
Norway died on the way to Scotland causing the
issue of who inherited the Scottish throne.

Marjorie Bruce	1296–1316, daughter of King Robert I and Isabella, married to Walter Stewart, mother of Robert II, the first Stewart monarch, during the Wars of Scottish Independence was imprisoned in a convent at Watton.
Mary Bruce	1282–1323, sister of King Robert I, held prisoner at Roxburgh Castle, first married Sir Neil Campbell and secondly Alexander Fraser of Touchfraser and Cowie.
Nigel Bruce	1279–1306, brother of King Robert I, taken prisoner and executed after the siege of Kildrummy Castle.
Patrick, 9th Earl of Dunbar	1285–1369, helped Edward II to escape from Dunbar Castle, signatory on the Declaration of Arbroath.
Philip IV	1268–1314, King of France 1285–1314.
Philip Moubray, Sir	died 1318 at the Battle of Faughart after changing sides to support Robert, Governor of Stirling Castle.
Reginald Crawford, Sir	Died 1307, appointed Sheriff of Ayr by the English.
Robert Boyd, Sir, 1st Lord of Kilmarnock	died 1333, rewarded after the Battle of Bannockburn with lands including Kilmarnock.
Robert de Bruce, 5th Lord Annandale	1215–95, grandfather of King Robert I.

Robert de Bruce, 6th Lord Annandale	1243–1304, father of King Robert I.
Robert the Bruce	1274–1329, King Robert I of Scotland 1306–29.
Robert Clifford, Sir	1274–1314, 1st Baron of Clifford, 1st Lord Warden of the Marches.
Thomas Bruce	1284–1307, brother of King Robert I.
Thomas, Earl of Lancaster	1278–1322, junior member of the house of Plantagenet, opposed his cousin Edward II.
Thomas Randolph, 1st Earl of Moray	1278–1332, nephew of King Robert I, later regent for King David II, signatory on the Declaration of Arbroath.
Walter Stewart, 6th High Steward of Scotland	1296–1327, married to Marjorie Bruce, father of King Robert II, also known as Walter the Steward, signatory on the Declaration of Arbroath.
William Wallace, Sir	1270–1305, was made joint Guardian of Scotland in 1297 with Sir Andrew Murray (older), known for being one of the main leaders during the Wars of Scottish Independence, he was murdered after a mock trial.
William, Earl of Ross	1274–1323, imprisoned King Robert I's wife, sister and daughter and other supporters in 1306, signatory on the Declaration of Arbroath.

MAPS OF
BANNOCKBURN

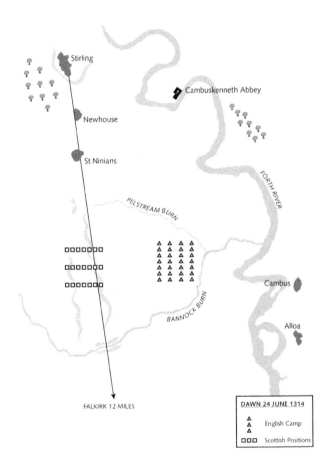

Stirling

Cambuskenneth Abbey

Newhouse

St Ninians

FORTH RIVER

PELSTREAM BURN

BANNOCK BURN

Cambus

Alloa

FALKIRK 12 MILES

DAWN 24 JUNE 1314

△
△   English Camp
△

☐☐☐ Scottish Positions

MAPS OF BANNOCKBURN

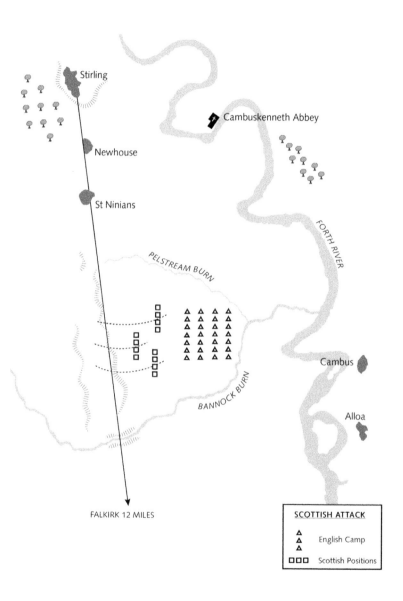

Stirling

Newhouse

St Ninians

Cambuskenneth Abbey

FORTH RIVER

PELSTREAM BURN

BANNOCK BURN

Cambus

Alloa

FALKIRK 12 MILES

SCOTTISH ATTACK

▲
▲   English Camp
▲

□□□   Scottish Positions

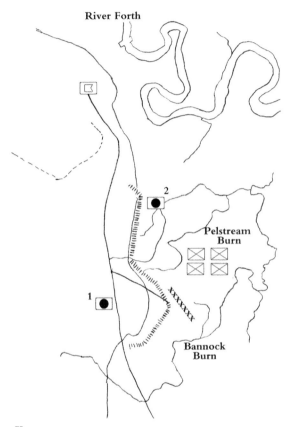

River Forth

Pelstream Burn

Bannock Burn

Key

⬜ Stirling Castle

● 23rd June: (1) Possible location of King Robert's 'Leding'
(2) Possible location of the Earl of Moray's fight

⊠ Possible concentration area of Edward II's army night of 23/24 June

||||| Likely extent of visibility toward the Scots line of approach of the English army coming from Falkirk and the English encampment

xxxx Possible direction of Scottish attack on 24 June

TIMELINE

March 1286   Death of Alexander III

1290   Death of Margaret, Maid of
                      Norway

1291–92   The Great Cause

1292   John Balliol inaugurated as King of
                      Scotland

October 1295   Franco–Scottish Treaty

April 1296   Edward I invades Scotland; the
                      Sacking of Berwick

July 1296   Edward deposes King John

Spring 1297   Rise of William Wallace

September 1297	Battle of Stirling Bridge
July 1298	Battle of Falkirk
February 1303	Battle of Roslin
1303	Franco–English Peace Agreement
1304	Strathord Agreement
August 1305	Execution of William Wallace
February 1306	Murder of John III Comyn
March 1306	Robert Bruce declares himself King of Scotland
June 1306	Battle of Methven
February 1307	Battle of Turnberry
April 1307	Battle of Glentrool
May 1307	Battle of Loudoun Hill
July 1307	Death of Edward I
May 1308	Battle of Inverurie

August 1308	Battle of Brander Pass
March 1309	Robert I's first parliament held at St Andrews
January 1312	Robert I captures Perth
October 1313	Edward II announces invasion of Scotland
March 1314	Fall of Edinburgh to the Scots
Lent 1314	Earl of Carrick negotiates surrender pact for Stirling Castle
23–24 June 1314	Battle of Bannockburn
Summer 1319	Battle of Myton
1320	Declaration of Arbroath
1327	Death of Edward II
1328	Treaty of Edinburgh–Northampton recognises Robert I as King of Scotland
7 June 1329	Death of King Robert I

GLOSSARY

Armati An 'armed' (armoured) soldier, also 'man-at-arms', vallet/vadlet and esquire

Bondi A serf or vilein, a person tied to the land

Burn A stream

Carse Land that is wet in winter and dry in summer

Charger A horse suitable for a man-at-arms

Comitiva The tenants and associates of a major landholder

Cottar A smallholder

Demesne	Property of a landholder kept in hand rather than rented out
Destrier	A superior charger
Flotilla	A group of ships
Grieve	A farm manager
Heriot	A sum paid on inheriting a tenancy
Hobelar	A mounted infantryman
Homines ad arm	See *armati*
Husbandman	Farm worker
Infeft	To be given a landholding
Infield land	Good-quality arable land
Knight service	Military obligation as a man-at-arms
Knights Templar	A military religious order, defunct after 1312
Merchet	A sum paid to a landlord when a tenant got married

Merk	160 pennies, 8 score (8 x 20) and coincidentally two thirds of £1 (240 pennies)
Mukkitland	See infield land
Nativi	A serf
Neyf	A serf
Paladin	A great warrior and leader
Peel	A palisade, a fortified camp and barracks rather than a castle
Phalanx	A body of spearmen
Reddendo	Rent due to the king or a superior
Rentier	One who rents land and then lets it out in smaller parcels for a profit
Restauro	Insurance for a charger or destrier
Runrig	Raised bed and ditch cultivation
Rustici	A serf

Schiltrom　　　A body of infantry

Servi　　　A serf

Slight　　　Damage to a castle making it indefensible

Tack　　　A farm lease

Thirl　　　An obligation to use the lord's mill
or other asset

Toun　　　A farm

Villein　　　A serf

FURTHER READING

A great deal of fine work on the life and times of Robert the Bruce has been published over the last fifty years, but the most important of them is Professor Barrow's great biography, which has the rare virtue of being both a very fine piece of scholarship and eminently easy to read – a difficult thing to achieve.

There are many good volumes and a great many that are best avoided, but I would suggest that this shortlist will provide most people with everything that they would ever want to know about King Robert and his kingdom and constitute a solid platform for those who want to conduct a more detailed study of his life and times:

Barbour, John (edited by A.A.M. Duncan), *The Bruce* (Edinburgh: Canongate Books Ltd, 1997).

Barrow, G.W.S., *Robert the Bruce and the Community of the Realm of Scotland* (Edinburgh: Edinburgh University Press, 2005).

Brown, Chris, *Bannockburn 1314* (Stroud: The History Press, 2009).

Brown, Michael, *The Black Douglases* (Edinburgh: John Donald
    Publishers Ltd, 2007).

Dixon, Piers, *Puir Labourers and Busy Husbandmen: The
    Medieval Countryside of Scotland 100–1600 (The Making of
    Scotland)* (Edinburgh: Birlinn Ltd, 2002).

Grant, A., *Independence and Nationhood: Scotland 1306–1469*
    (Edinburgh: Edinburgh University Press, 1991).

Nicholson, R., *Edinburgh History of Scotland: In The Later Middle
    Ages* (Edinburgh: Mercat Press, 1986).

Prestwich, Michael, *Plantagenet England: 1225–1360* (Oxford:
    OUP, 2005).

Watson, Fiona, *Under the Hammer: Edward I and Scotland,
    1286–1307* (Edinburgh: John Donald Publishers Ltd, 2009).

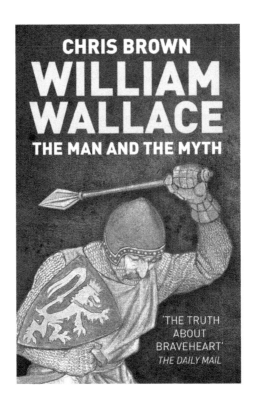

978 0 7509 5387 0

The destination for history
www.thehistorypress.co.uk